# The Tall Ships of Today
## in Photographs

Frank O. Braynard

DOVER PUBLICATIONS, INC.
*New York*

*This book is dedicated to my wife Doris and
to two special friends who helped so much—
Bob and Rhoda Amon*

Copyright © 1993 by Frank O. Braynard.
All rights reserved under Pan American and International Copyright
Conventions.

Published in Canada by General Publishing Company, Ltd., 30 Lesmill Road,
Don Mills, Toronto, Ontario.

Published in the United Kingdom by Constable and Company, Ltd., 3 The
Lanchesters, 162–164 Fulham Palace Road, London W6 9ER.

*The Tall Ships of Today in Photographs* is a new work, first published by
Dover Publications, Inc., in 1993.

Manufactured in the United States of America
Dover Publications, Inc., 31 East 2nd Street, Mineola, N.Y. 11501

*Library of Congress Cataloging-in-Publication Data*

Braynard, Frank Osborn, 1916–
      The tall ships of today in photographs / Frank O. Braynard.
            p.      cm.
      ISBN 0-486-27163-3 (pbk.)
      1. Sailing ships—Pictorial works. I. Title.
VM307.B68  1993
387.2′2′0222—dc20                                                        93-18442
                                                                                      CIP

# Contents

## PRIVATE VESSELS

# Introduction

Steamships, not sailing vessels, have always been my interest. One day in 1961, I got a call from the Coast Guard's Public Information Officer, Ed Duenzel, who told me about a man with an idea—Nils Hansell, who worked for IBM. A day or two later Hansell walked into my office, an enthusiastic smile on his face. He said, "Wouldn't it be fun to have all the world's tall ships in New York harbor at the same time?" From that moment on great sailing craft have occupied much of my time.

There is no doubt that Nils Hansell had a tremendous influence on me. Sad to say, he died in 1990. Nils taught me a great deal—about living, about how important enthusiasm was and about being persistent, determined and always optimistic. The editor of one of the house organs of IBM, he was an outgoing person, a man of ideas. But he had more: He acted on his ideas. He had a way of making contacts who helped him make his dreams happen. I am glad that I took him seriously. When Nils proposed his tall-ship idea, I was working for the Moran Towing & Transportation Co. My office was on the twenty-fifth floor of 17 Battery Place, the best location anyone interested in ships could have. My room looked out on the magnificent harbor. I could see it all, from the Statue of Liberty in the immediate foreground, out to the Narrows. My predecessor in the job had sat with his back to this magnificent view. My first act when I became editor of *Tow Line,* the Moran house magazine, and public-relations director for the world's largest tug company, was to turn the desk around so I faced the harbor. The ten years I spent there were among the happiest of my life. But when I look back, all my jobs were great fun—the 17 years I spent with the American Merchant Marine Institute, a trade association where I did public relations for 80 ship lines; the four years as ship-news reporter on the *New York Herald Tribune;* the four years with the South Street Seaport Museum, not to mention my 15 years with the American Merchant Marine Museum, where I am in the midst of a host of exciting projects.

## Early Helpers

Nils Hansell and I sat down in my Moran office soon after I met him and we coined the name "Operation Sail" (later also known as "OpSail"). I began writing to countries that owned tall ships and used them as training vessels, and to any other group that operated tall ships. I started a newsletter and began putting one out every month to keep all who responded aware of what was happening.

Fortunately for me, Admiral Edmond J. Moran, head of the towing firm bearing his family name, was enthusiastic. At this point I had a number of good friends in key positions who were eager to help. There was that grand old man of the sea we knew as "Smiling Jack"—John Bayliss. In the Great War he had been responsible for taking the *Vaterland* (later renamed *Leviathan*). When the United States entered World War II, he had risen to be Captain of the Port of New York for the Coast Guard, and he had seized the *Normandie.* He knew everyone and opened many doors for me.

In no time we had a committee, with many friendly helpers. We got tremendous help from Robert Hubner, Senior Vice President of IBM. Still another wonderful associate of those early days was H. Alexander Salm, world-known yachting personality and Incres Line executive. Our first chairman was Rear Admiral John J. Bergen. Walter S. Gubelmann was of great help raising funds. Enos Curtin, Brad A. Warner, Lewis A. Lapham all advised on money matters, each lending great prestige. Julian ("Dooley") K. Roosevelt and F. Briggs Dalzell were key supporters. Captain William K. Earle, master of the *Eagle,* and Harry Nilsson offered seasoned council.

The concept of Operation Sail was so exciting, so genuine that it drew people to it from the start. I gave hundreds of talks, sometimes as many as three a day, before every kind of group. For me there emerged a genuine rationale, something that I reallly believed in and that I could project with sincerity. It was simple. I know that seamen are a very special kind of people. Because of their work they are continually meeting others from many different lands. Becoming international citizens, they know how to live with "foreigners." They learn immediately that the very word "foreigner" is unfortunate. In no time those we think of as "foreigners" become friends. It follows, quite naturally, that we should all be like seamen. After all, we are all seamen on spaceship Earth. With this concept, which I sincerely believe to be true, I succeeded beyond my wildest dreams.

## Michael Forrestal

A major break for us came when Nils somehow got to know Michael Forrestal, son of James V. Forrestal, the famous political figure of the Kennedy era. Michael Forrestal showed us his card and we were greatly impressed, as it gave his office location as "the White House, Washington, D.C." He urged us to visit him and said

President Kennedy agrees to become Patron of OpSail. (The author is in the background, to the right of the President.)

he would arrange an interview with President Kennedy. Our hope was to persuade the President to be our patron. At this juncture we had another vitally important break, out of the blue. When it became known via the IBM grapevine that Nils and I were hoping to meet the President, we received a call from the office of IBM President Tom Watson. He asked us who our spokesman was going to be. The most important person we had managed to get involved was Admiral George Wauchope, President of Farrell Lines. Tom said we must have someone who knows "Jack." He picked up the telephone and dialed. (I understand that top IBMers always dial their own phone calls.) Someone answered and Nils and I both heard Tom Watson say, "Hi, Bus—I have two 'kooks' here with me. They have a date to see Jack, and I would like you to go with them." Not only did the famous America's Cup hero, Emil ("Bus") Mosbacher, go with us to Washington, but we flew down in Watson's own private jet. More than that, "Bus" Mosbacher agreed, after some heavy pleading on the telephone, to be the Chairman of OpSail, a post he has held ever since.

### Meeting President Kennedy

The White House meeting with the President was all we could possibly have hoped for. Even the hour's wait outside the Oval Office was a dream come true. With us, waiting, were the Secretary of the Navy, the Commandant of the U.S. Coast Guard, Michael Forrestal and several other high personages. We had agreed among our five-man committee that only "Bus" Mosbacher would do the talking. Our very brief request that the President be our Patron was written down on a slip of paper and in "Bus"'s pocket. Our group was ushered into the Oval Office.

After introductions had been made, "Bus" reached for the slip of paper and started to open his mouth. But President Kennedy interrupted him. With a warm smile, he said, "Just a minute, I want you to see a superb bone model of an old ship that was just given to me." He hurried us all over to a corner of the office and stood beside the model. "Bus" spoke briefly about its beauty, age and style. The rest of us just listened. Again "Bus" tried to speak and, again, the President put him off, taking us over to see a painting of a ship hanging on a wall. The President's obvious interest in sail and sailing came through clearly. We admired the picture and then the President said he had another "original" we must see in the next room. Here I got an insight into this remarkable man and his great strength as a politician. He opened the door and ushered us into what turned out to be the Cabinet Room. Two or three people were sitting at a long table. President Kennedy introduced our group before showing us the painting. When we returned to the Oval Office, "Bus" got out his paper and asked President Kennedy to be our Patron. The President said he would be glad to. We all shook hands and left.

## An Embarrassing Moment

Our first embarrassment, from which we learned much, involved the *Eagle*. My work at the American Merchant Marine Institute (before Moran) had involved an annual visit to Chicago to attend a trade convention. On such occasions it was my job to get to know as many important people as I could. I had an expense account so I could take such "wheels" to dinner. On one such occasion I became friends with Admiral Chester A. Richmond, Commandant of the U.S. Coast Guard. I told him about OpSail and asked him if we could count on the *Eagle,* which, as host ship, would lead the parade of tall ships into New York harbor. He said we could, and I let it go at that—an error, as I later discovered, when I had a telephone call from the Coast Guard Academy at New London, where the *Eagle* was berthed. The Academy, it seemed, knew nothing of what we planned to do with their square-rigger. Commodore Bayliss and I responded with rapidity.

We went to New London, apologized for having failed to let them know all about OpSail and did our best to patch things up. Having the help of "Smiling Jack," who considered all officers in the Coast Guard as "his boys," was a tremendous break. (He had sailed around the world on a square-rigger in 1904.) At our New London session we met Admiral Willard J. Smith, Superintendent of the Coast Guard Academy. As we were chatting, an idea occurred to me and it helped. I mentioned that there was to be a tall-ship meeting in London within a couple of months. I saw his eyes light up. I added that he should go to it.. The OpSail committee did not have enough money for me to make the trip but a few days later I got a telephone call from Admiral Smith to tell me he had received approval from Admiral Richmond to go to London, adding that he would go in a Coast Guard seaplane (with wheels). He asked if I would like to go with him.

It was a remarkable experience. Our plane could land on either land or sea. We stopped for the first night at Gander, Newfoundland. During the flight, whenever we passed over a Coast Guard base or vessel, the Admiral radioed his compliments. We got the red carpet, literally and figuratively. In London we met with the Sail Training Association, who agreed to run a transatlantic race from Plymouth to New York, via Bermuda, prior to OpSail. The noted ship master-author, Alan Villiers, who usually turned up his nose at government-owned sail-training ships, came from his home in Oxford to meet with us. The idea of several thousand sailors coming together for the event must have won him over. I met him again later, when he brought the replica of the *Mayflower* to America.

## John Masefield

A coincidence led me to another great name at this point. I was a Village Trustee in my hometown of Sea Cliff, New York. As low man on the totem pole, I was put in charge of public relations, trees and dogs. One day a lady called me with a complaint that her dog had been bothered by one off his leash. She was the wife of a friend, Sam McCoy, well-known local author of *Nor Death Dismay,* which told the story of men and ships of the American Export Line in World War II. I went over to their home and sat on their front porch, letting Mrs. McCoy tell me all about the incident. As I had hoped, Sam eventually came out onto the porch and I was able to shift the subject to tall ships and told him about OpSail. His eyes lit up and he told me he had an idea. Fifty years before, he said, he had been a bartender in Philadelphia. Serving drinks with him was a Britisher who loved the sea and ships and who was even then a fine poet—he was, in fact, John Masefield. Sam added that he had kept up with Masefield, who had become Poet Laureate of England. He encouraged me to write him and gave me his home address—

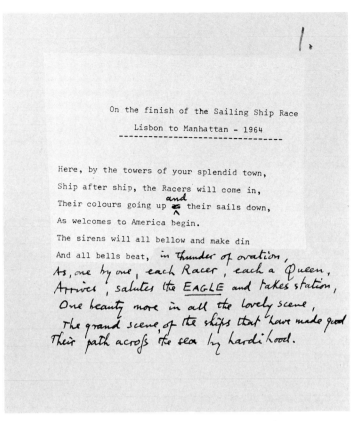

Part of the original manuscript of the poem written by John Masefield for OpSail.

maybe Masefield would dedicate one of his older poems to the concept of brotherhood of the sea and OpSail. By then I had learned to try for the seemingly impossible and so I wrote. In no time I got a lovely hand-written letter: Masefield would be happy to dedicate an old poem, but wouldn't I prefer a few original verses? The new work was entitled "On the Finish of the Sailing Ship Race/Lisbon to Manhattan—1964":

> Here, by the towers of your splendid town,
> Ship after ship, the Racers will come in,
> Their colours going up and their sails down,
> As welcomes to America begin.
> The sirens will all bellow and make din
> And all bells beat, in thunder of ovation,
> As, one by one, each Racer, each a Queen,
> Arrives, salutes the *Eagle* and takes station,
> One beauty more in all the lovely scene,
> The grand scene, of the ships that have made good
> Their path across the sea by hardihood.
>
> Ah, would that he who helped to plan this test
> Of manhood on the sea, were with us still,*
> Watching, with us, the ending of the quest,
> As men and ships their destinies fulfil.
> He whom America in desolation
> Now mourns, from sea to sea; but he has gone
> A Nation's memory and veneration,
> Among the radiant, ever venturing on,
> Somewhere, with morning, as such spirits will.

This poem has been quoted in many publications. In my files, perhaps the most treasured reminder of tall ships that I possess, are the original draft and six letters from John Masefield.

*A reference to the assassination of President Kennedy.

## Prince Philip

Again and again as we organized OpSail, Nils Hansell showed that his gift of gall brought amazing results. For example, he wrote to Prince Philip and asked him to be a Patron. I laughed at the idea, but a couple of months later, to my amazement, we were both invited to lunch with the Prince at the Mansion House, London. OpSail had no funds, so my wife Doris and I decided to go to England third class on the S.S. *United States*, taking our two children, David and Noelle. While they went to Windsor Castle I went to the Mansion House, where I found that 200 other people were also to have lunch with Prince Philip. In fact, the seating list was almost three feet long. At first I thought I saw my name, misspelled, assigned to a table near the back of the large hall. But someone corrected me, pointing out that my name, properly spelled, showed that I was on the dais, only three places away from Prince Philip. On my left was Lord Besborough, who, my informant noted, owned half of London. To my right was Harold Rupert Leofric George Alexander, the Earl of Tunis and General Montgomery's boss in North Africa in 1942. Being assigned to the dais entitled me to go into a reception room where the dais guests were to be lined up in accordance with their order of seating at the head table. As I approached the door to this room a magnificently uniformed factotum asked my name. He turned, thumped a huge staff on the wooden floor and intoned my name as it had never been intoned before and, doubtless, never will be again. The only sad thing for me was that I was the first person in the room and the only one to hear it.

Gradually, more people came into the hall and one very distinguished-looking Englishman began to talk with me. He said, "You must be the person from New York." I nodded. He went on, "My great-great-great-great-grandfather captured that city. My name is Howe." (His ancestor was William Howe.) Suddenly I noticed that Howe was giving me the "pickled eye." Anyone who has been given the pickled eye will know what I mean—a pickled eye is a clear and positive indication that you are doing something very wrong. I sensed it—and turned to discover Prince Philip, smiling and extending his hand toward me over the back of a couch. Apparently, I had been introduced to him, but it had all, somehow, gone over my head. I regrouped. Quickly I reached out for his hand, shook it and said: "We hope you will be our Patron for Operation Sail 1964, at New York." He gave a big smile and said, "Certainly." The functionaries got us all in the right order, we heard the band in the dining hall strike up "God Save the Queen," and in we paraded.

## Getting the Danmark

But not everything was smooth sailing. In fact, when I look back at it, I believe it might well be said that every ship on our list turned us down at first. The *Danmark*, the Danish training ship used to teach youngsters to be sailors, was a case in point. Danish Consul General Krogmeyer, in New York, seemed, at the start, to be very interested and offered to host a large cocktail party for us in his apartment, allowing us to invite up to 50 people. It was a grand success and I thanked him profusely. Then came the bombshell. The Consul General looked sad and added, "Of course, the *Danmark* can't be here." When I asked him why, he replied that she was scheduled to be dry-docked in Copenhagen in July. At about this time, Robert Moses gave our small committee $2000, which Nils Hansell and I divided, each of us going to visit different ships in Europe. My first stop was at Copenhagen, and I was able to convince authorities to hold up the dry-docking of the *Danmark* and schedule the ship's visit to New York for OpSail.

The *Danmark*'s master was one of the most famous in all the tall-ship fraternity. His name was Hansen and he was overjoyed at

the prospect of coming to New York with other tall ships for our event. But he suffered a serious heart attack and his doctor advised against the long Atlantic voyage. His daughter, however, was also a doctor, and he persuaded her to sail with him. When he entered New York, his was the only ship that tacked her way against contrary winds through the Narrows and up to the Battery. Once the ship was safely at her pier, Captain Hansen had another heart attack. He had to let someone else take the ship home and remained in New York for some time to recover. To celebrate his return to health, I entertained him at the famous King Cole room in the St. Regis Hotel. The *Danmark* has never missed an Operation Sail since.

## David Rockefeller

Henry R. Geyelin, a special assistant to David Rockefeller, was one of our most important sources of strength in the early days of this, our first OpSail. I remember seeing with awe Mr. Rockefeller's posh office at the top of the then new Chase Manhattan building in lower Manhattan. There, leaning against a wall unhung, was an oil painting that he had just bought, a glorious work portraying pebbles under a few inches of water right at the edge of a beach. I believe it was by Alfred Sisley.

The contact gave us one of the most brilliant OpSail events. Through Harry Geyelin's "pull" we were given the privilege of holding a party at the top of the Chase Manhattan tower a few days before OpSail. But the thing I remember best was a crazy little moment before the party began, involving a high-speed express elevator on the ground floor. Everyone seemed to be arriving at once—there were uniforms and gold stripes everywhere. Doris and I approached an elevator packed with brass. They squeezed back to give just enough room for Doris to get in. She did. I watched the arrow indicate the progress of the elevator up, and then watched it heading down. A moment or so later its door opened. There stood Doris, an embarrassed smile on her lovely face. Behind her was the same packed mass of admirals, captains and others—all looking very awkward. Apparently the door had opened at the sixtieth floor, but the crowd was too slow in getting off and the door had closed. The whole crowd had sped down again. As everyone grinned the door again closed. The next time the elevator returned empty.

## July 14, 1964

The first OpSail took place on July 14, 1964. We had 11 Class A tall ships and 12 Class B. Millions saw it, but our advance publicity had been minimal and, to most people, it came as a complete surprise. We had prepared a grand little spiral-bound program with shiny blue covers. Unfortunately, we had neglected to get peddler licenses and our volunteers who were selling the programs were harassed by the police. It was entirely our fault; we sold only a few of the programs. But they were stored away on Pier A at the Battery and were used a few years later.

I started a new project—an effort to save the Custom House. An outstanding example of Beaux-Arts architecture, it has been preserved. This work was interrupted when Peter Stanford told me of his new campaign to restore some of the ancient buildings just below the Brooklyn Bridge at the bottom of Fulton Street. He called his dream the South Street Seaport Museum. I was interested and worked as a volunteer from the beginning. In 1970 I left Moran to work full-time for Peter and the Seaport, which is today the largest tourist attraction in Manhattan. I became Program Director for the Seaport and never enjoyed anything more. Peter added his voice to those of others. "You must do another tall-ship event," he kept saying. The idea of making it a part of the nation's Bicentennial clicked, and we were off and running.

## The Bicentennial

The 1976 OpSail proved to be one of the biggest events that ever took place in New York City. It came at a time when the city was struggling to survive, and many have credited the stimulus that OpSail 1976 gave New York for turning the fortunes of the city around. Six million people came into New York to see it, and it was far bigger than the first—in fact people have said that it was the most successful such event ever run in New York before or since. We had over 150 vessels. The team that ran this OpSail included many from 1964, such as George L. "Tim" Peirce from the Port of New York Authority. Also aboard were Roger Fortin of IBM, Alexander Lyon, Howard Slotnick, Henry Geyelin, Alec Salm, Ellen Isbrandtsen Sykes and John S. Fullerton, to mention only a few. As usual, we started without any funds. This time we ended over $700,000 in the black. Just as the Bicentennial OpSail was getting started, Peter Stanford and I were trying to get the National Council for Historic Preservation to save old and historic ships. They would have none of it. But when they saw the mass of money earned by OpSail 1976, they quickly changed their minds and the shipping division was created. We gave them $300,000. The rest went to help the South Street Seaport Museum.

## How the 1976 OpSail Began

In 1972 Doris and I went to Kiel to see tall ships gathered in that ancient German port. It was a joy to see America's *Eagle* docked just behind Poland's *Dar Pomorza,* the first Iron-Curtain tall ship to come out of her own waters and join a European gathering of tall ships. Captain Ed Cassidy, of the *Eagle,* introduced us to the master of the Polish ship. We had coffee in his handsome wardroom and worked out a deal whereby the *Dar Pomorza* would come to New York in 1976 if the *Eagle* went to Gdynia in 1974, when Poland was having their own Operation Sail. Everything seemed settled and we were pleased that, in a small way, we were helping to break down the division between East and West. However, Dr. Henry Kissinger did not see things that way. Showing off his great knowledge, he pontificated that the United States had never signed Poland's Lublin Convention (which no one else seemed to have heard of) at the end of World War II. So, he reasoned, the *Eagle,* a government-owned ship, could not participate. Then someone suggested that, if we could not have the *Eagle,* we should try to get Rudy Schaefer's replica of the schooner-yacht *America* to go to Gdynia. She had frequently docked at South Street Seaport Museum and I had gotten to know Rudy Schaefer. I started on this tack only to discover that Rudy had sold the ship to someone named Presley Blake. By this time I knew how important it was to tell your difficulties to everyone. I began to talk up the *America* problem. My brother-in-law, Arthur W. Peabody, Jr., to whom I unburdened myself one day, laughed and said, "Presley Blake was my roommate at Duke University. He owns Friendly Ice Cream Co."

## The Dar Pomorza

So I called Blake up and got an interview. I wailed and stamped around his office and wrung my hands and he agreed to send the *America* to Poland in 1974. I decided to go too, with my own funds, of course, as OpSail had no money. From start to finish I had great

President Ford with the author at the Bicentennial OpSail.

help from Polish author Jerzy Wadowski, of Warsaw. He began by urging me to fly with LOT, Polish Airlines. Jerzy then advised me to find out who the captain of the plane was going to be and to get to know him. I did, learning in the process that he had a two-year-old daughter. This gave Jerzy another good idea: Get a present for the daughter. I did. Then, when I found that I could not go on the day I had picked and had to change my reservations, the airline captain called to say that he was changing his schedule so he could continue to help personally. More than that, he invited me to spend our first night in Warsaw at his home. I have rarely enjoyed such hospitality. The next morning they drove me to the airport and I flew the relatively short distance to Gdynia, Poland's famous seaport.

## The Kruzenshtern

I stayed in a small hotel within sight of the port. That night was terrible—I had no watch and could not find one in the entire hotel. so I did not dare to go to sleep. I had been invited to see the parade of tall ships from the decks of the great four-master *Kruzenshtern,* and had to get to the pier at 5 A.M. So I just nodded, watching Venus go across the horizon from one side of my window to the other as the long night wore on. It was bleak and cold as I trudged to the pier, but the sight of the many tall masts urged me on. I clambered aboard the *Kruzenshtern* and looked her over. As I was getting to know her commodious Liverpool deck amidships, a friendly face appeared. "Welcome," the stranger said, with a cordial handshake.

"My name is Anatoly Chesnokov. I heard you were coming and am sure you would like a little breakfast. Follow me." How different everything was as we sat in the officers' mess and drank steaming hot chocolate. The huge hunks of brown bread loaded with fresh butter tasted like the finest pastry. Captain Chesnokov looked and even acted like the actor Ronald Colman. We remained fast friends until his death in 1991. After breakfast he asked me down to his cabin. As he opened the door I saw from the bottles on his desk that it was to be a crisis situation for me. Drinking is not my forte. In fact I can't stand the taste of anything alcoholic. However, after two small glasses of vodka I saw a way out. In walked the ship's bandmaster, who spoke fair English. I asked him if he could whistle the wonderful main theme from Shostakovich's Seventh ("Leningrad") Symphony. I whistled it to make sure he knew what I was talking about. He nodded his head several times with a huge grin and whistled it back to me. I whistled another variation to him and we exchanged bows and smiles. We continued with this jolly exchange in a hundred variations. I was saved. You cannot drink while you whistle.

The parade of sail that day was tremendous. I made dozens of quick pen sketches, many of which I later used in my book *Search for the Tall Ships*. It was a wonderful event and the replica *America* was the hit of the show. Presley Blake was there, basking in the glory of his private yacht. Now that I had managed to have an American-flag tall ship go to Poland, I had every right to hope that I could persuade the Polish Maritime Academy to send the *Dar Pomorza* to America for 1976. Our contact was a Captain Dr. Duda, who headed the Academy and spoke for the Polish tall ship. Before flying to Poland, I had written to him inviting him to attend a reception aboard the *America*. In anticipation of this, I spent money we did not have by ordering our first Operation Sail flag from the Annin flag company. I designed a very simple pennant and ordered just one. I told the company that it would undoubtedly have countless orders for more, and it willingly made this first one. It was red, white and blue, with red letters "OpSail—'76" on white and a blue border. I took the pennant with me and presented it on the decks of the *America*. My friend was editor of the one major Polish magazine of the sea, *Morza*. While I made a little speech and gave the pennant to Dr. Duda, he photographed the maritime academy head accepting it and promptly published the picture with a rousing story about Poland having accepted the OpSail flag. The participation of the *Dar Pomorza* was assured. Not only did *Dar Pomorza* come, but with her came three smaller Polish tall ships.

### The Other Polish Tall Ships

Of the three smaller Polish ships that came to New York for OpSail, two decided to detour to Chicago before returning home, for the city has a very large Polish-American population. The Coast Guard had a rule that any Iron Curtain ship would have to request permission to call at any American port a week in advance. When OpSail was over, these three smaller Polish ships sailed to Chicago via the St. Lawrence River, stopping at many cities along the way, with a huge party at every stop. In Chicago the Polish officers and crews were welcomed by Mayor Daley.

After Chicago two of the ships returned home via New Orleans, passing down the length of the Mississippi River. The third ship had a special purpose in coming. After her three-day stay at New York for the Bicentennial, she headed south for the port of Savannah, Georgia. A container of Polish earth the ship had brought was placed on the grave of Casimir Pulaski, who was killed in Savannah while commanding both the French and the American cavalry in the siege of the city during the American Revolution.

### Across the Channel

After my visit to Gdynia I went to Portsmouth, England, arriving in a small steamer. The Sail Training Association had planned another tall-ship event in the British Channel, with the same ships that had sailed into Gdynia participating. I was happy to see the *Kruzenshtern* again, and I made a sketch of the bows of the *Dar Pomorza*, *Kruzenshtern* and the *Tovarisch*. At this point I was joined by Howard Slotnick, an automobile salesman from the Bronx deeply interested in South Street Seaport and tall ships, and a member of our OpSail Board. We knew the *Kruzenshtern* was to sail to France across the English Channel after the review and we were dying to be aboard her. It was only a 70-mile trip, and I assumed it would take only one day. I found Chesnokov and asked him about our chances of sailing aboard his great ship. He went to Captain Snyder and put in a good word for us and we were welcomed aboard and given a cabin. The trip to France actually took two nights and three days, and we enjoyed it to the hilt. We sailed and very slowly started out into the Channel. Howard and I ate with the deck officers in their mess. The next morning we were told more about the plan for the day. The Royal Yacht *Britannia* would be anchored and take the review. Major tall ships included the *Dar Pomorza*, *Sir Winston Churchill*, *Amerigo Vespucci* and *Kruzenshtern*. As we were the largest of the reviewing fleet, we came at the very end.

The review was one of the most colorful and dramatic events that I have ever witnessed. The day was perfect and hundreds of small boats were on hand to sail along with us and watch. I made a particularly difficult sketch standing on the forecastle, with the beginning of the highly steeved bowsprit in the immediate foreground. All the while I heard two Soviet midshipmen behind me working hard. I turned to see what they were doing and found that they were being taught how to make a wire splice. And it was very difficult work—their fingers were bloody.

Later, Howard and I were told that Captain Snyder wanted to see us in the ship's wardroom. Someone had made elaborate preparations for the session—on one side of the table American and Soviet flags were crossed at the places for six or seven of the ship's officers. The same preparations had been made for Howard and me on the other side. After a few opening comments, the ship's interpreter said that Captain Snyder had a question. His comment was protracted, leading me to wonder if he was expressing regret that the ship could not come to OpSail. The interpreter then took over, "The Captain wants to know if you will help him get new sails." It was true that the *Kruzenshtern*'s sails were darkish and seemed somewhat stained. We assured him that we could easily find companies that could make new sails for the great ship, but the Soviets never found the money to buy them. The ship came to OpSail, however, dirty sails and all, and we were overjoyed to have her.

We drank tea throughout the voyage. On the third day, as we were approaching St. Malo, I was chatting with someone on the Liverpool deck. As usual, several Soviet crew members were standing nearby. I mentioned how I would love to have some coffee. One of the seamen recognized the word coffee. He beckoned me to follow him and led me below to his cabin. As I entered, he dropped to his knees before a built-in drawer. He opened it and pulled out a can of Soviet instant coffee. We shook hands and I thanked him as best I could. I have never opened that can of coffee, which remains, to this day, one of my favorite mementos of OpSail 1976.

### Winter Visit to Moscow

Pinning down the Soviet Ministry of Fisheries and getting the *Kruzenshtern* to come to New York took a lot more letter writing and telephoning. A visit I made to Moscow in the middle of winter in 1975 clinched it. The trip, with all its feel of a cloak-and-dagger spy rendezvous, was quickly arranged between me and the Soviet Naval Attaché in Washington. I got the dates set even before I had a visa, but the Attaché assured me that would be no problem—he would send it on by air courier and have it delivered to me in London. Exactly *where* would be confirmed by telephone. I flew to London, stayed in my hotel and waited for the call, which, in fact, came. The Soviet London office offered to deliver the visa. For reasons unknown, their messenger brought it to me at a big drugstore near my hotel. I stood waiting there for half an hour until the man with a Russian fur hat came. That was how I was to recognize him. He gave me a little packet and hurried off. I found my visa inside with some maps and a hotel reservation. There was also a note asking me to wait for further instructions in the main waiting room of the Moscow airport.

When I got to Russia, the airport waiting room was packed with several hundred people, all waiting patiently in long rows of seats. I started toward the back wondering how many hours it would take for me to get up to the front spot. Instead, someone came by and asked if I was the Operation Sail person. I said yes and he told me to follow him. I hurried after him to the front entrance of the airport where a black limousine with chauffeur was waiting. I got in and we made what seemed like a very long drive into the outskirts of the city. As we passed a large monument, the driver told me it was a five-times-life-size tank trap marking the closest point the invading Germans had come to entering the city during the war. Eventually we came to a fine big hotel. I was helped out, given a room and found a sheaf of papers and maps on the bureau with full instructions for meetings to be held the following day. After a good night's sleep, I had breakfast in the hotel dining room and did not bother to go back to my room—there was the chauffeured black limousine out front waiting for me, so I just stepped in and we were off. It was not until we had been driving for half an hour that I realized I did not have my maps, instructions and other materials. However the driver knew that I was going first to the Ministry of Fisheries, an old wooden building that looked as if it must have been built in the time of the czars. I entered and headed for an elevator. A figure swathed in a thick scarf and greatcoat rushed toward the same elevator, which we entered together. He turned out to be Captain Kosteskyi, First Officer of the *Kruzenshtern.* We sat down at a long table in a conference room. Across from me were a whole string of uniformed Soviet officers. During the long session, every kind of question was asked: How would they dispose of the ships' garbage? Would there be good piers, where, what kind, with "camels" (floats that keep a ship from coming too close to a pier)? Would there be entertainment for the cadets, the officers and crews? After about two hours of such questions, old Captain Borisoff, who had asked most of the questions in a very stern voice, relaxed. He looked at me and his face broke into a huge smile. "We want very much to come," he said, and the meeting was over.

My limousine then took me to the Ministry of the Merchant Marine and I had another equally cordial session. After that I ended the day with a visit to the American consulate. My mission to Moscow was accomplished.

## Other Tall Ships

Getting the *Kruzenshtern* was one of the main successes of my trips around the world in 1974 and 1975. We had relatively little difficulty in persuading the *Tovarisch,* Russia's other major sail-training ship, to come. She was one of five German-built sister ships, the others being Romania's *Mircea,* Portugal's *Sagres,* Germany's *Gorch Fock* and our own *Eagle.* I had learned of these "five sisters" from a conversation with my neighbor and fellow

Long Island Rail Road commuter Charlie Hurley. He was a continuous source of help and I owe much to his enthusiasm and knowledge for the success of OpSail 1964 and 1976.

A Romanian-American shoe manufacturer–salesman who had an office in New York gave us all the leads that led to *Mircea's* coming. Romania was so poor at the time that the ship sailed without enough fuel to complete the trip. So, in another illustration of how tall ships create international friendship, the U.S. Navy refueled the ship, in total secrecy, in mid-Atlantic. This story never came out. The *Sagres* provided another example of the goodwill engendered by tall ships for, despite the fact that Portuguese-American relations were at a low point, Dr. Theotonio Pereia, the Portuguese ambassador, invited Nils Hansell and me to Lisbon to discuss the participation of the *Sagres.* I was unable to accept the kind invitation, but Nils went and the *Sagres* has been a participant in the four OpSails held in New York since then.

## German Participation

Germany's *Gorch Fock* had originally turned us down. I had a very good relationship with the *Journal of Commerce.* Knowing that Erik Ridder, the paper's publisher, was of German extraction, I went to him for help. He told me that the *Journal* would be willing to publish an editorial piece, written by me, stressing that the gathering of tall ships was an event of worldwide importance and that any country that had a tall ship but was not represented would regret it. My editorial was carried on the front page of that famous commercial daily and in two months we got word that the *Gorch Fock* was coming.

At least one German should be eternally grateful to us for this participation—the ship's young third officer, Hans von Stackelburg, later to be her master. He has told me that, when the *Gorch Fock* did come to New York, a young secretary from the German Consulate was among the large German party visiting the ship. The young lady was introduced to the third officer. They fell in love and were later married. When he became commander of the ship, Captain von Stackelburg made sure that a small brass marker was put on the ship's deck at the spot where this first meeting took place.

## Japan

The Japanese had two great tall ships but we continually received negative responses to all our invitations. In 1975 I determined to go to Japan. My former roommate at Duke, Nobakazu Fukuhara (known to me as "Nick"), had risen to head one of the largest Japanese companies, and was famous worldwide. We had met several times since Duke and when I told him of my hopes for Japanese participation he urged Doris and me to come to his country, generously offering to pay all our expenses while we were in his land. I was able to travel on the Royal Viking Line as a lecturer on an eastbound transpacific trip from Kobe. So our only costs would involve the flights to Tokyo and home from San Francisco. When we got off the plane in Japan there was Nick, waving from behind the barriers. He had two cars—one for us, the other for our baggage.

Although we were received with every courtesy by the Ministry of Transportation, their answer to our request was always the same: Sorry, the two tall ships need new sails, new decks and the Ministry's budget is too small. The American Ambassador, James Hodgson received us cordially. We persevered with various talks and visited other key people whose names had been given to us by Hisashi Noma, a Japanese author I knew. One morning Ambassador Hodgson called to tell that he had decided to invite the

Japanese Minister of Foreign Affairs, adding that he was going to tell him that OpSail was a worldwide event of such importance that Japan would lose face were it not represented. It worked. Several days later, the leading Tokyo papers had pictures of the *Nippon Maru* on their front pages, making known that she was going to New York in 1976. She came, the necessary repairs having been made. After the event was over, the ship's master, Captain Hashimoto, came to my office in the World Trade Center, bringing with him several associates from the ship. They carried a large package. I accepted it with thanks and we opened it. As I admired its contents, a large photo of the *Nippon Maru* framed in heavy teak, Captain Hashimoto said, "You helped us get a new deck and we thought you would like to have a piece of the old one. This picture is framed in teak from the *Nippon Maru*." It is moments such as this that have made my participation in the organization of OpSail so rewarding.

## A Recap and a Look to the Future

There have been, at this writing, four OpSails in New York. The first was held in 1964. The next, held in 1976, honored the American Bicentennial. On July 4, 1986, an Operation Sail marked the centennial of the unveiling of the Statue of Liberty. We had more ships than in 1976 but the event lacked the excitement of 1976. Although President Reagan was there and even more ships came than in 1976, the 1986 tall-ships gathering at New York never generated the extraordinary enthusiasm and public participation of the Bicentennial. On July 4, 1992, there was the fourth OpSail. Once again there were even more tall ships, but this event also failed to match 1976. There are plans for a somewhat different tall-ship event, Americas' Sail, in 1994, and there are serious thoughts of a fifth OpSail in the year 2000, indicating that the romantic allure of tall ships is likely to last into the new millennium.

# Museum Ships

# *Balclutha*

Built in Scotland in 1886, the *Balclutha* is the proud centerpiece of San Francisco's waterfront. For her first 13 years the great ship served worldwide, carrying coal from Cardiff, whiskey from London and guano from Iquique. Then, bought by the Alaska Packers' Association and renamed *Star of Alaska,* she took cannery workers north and brought salmon back to San Francisco. Her third career was a sad one: She was run up and down the coast of California as a "pirate ship" for tourists. Towed to San Francisco, she was laid up and abandoned on the mud flats.

The ship was the first of a notable series of great sailing ships saved by Karl Kortum, founder and for years head man at the San Francisco Maritime Museum. In 1954, Mr. Kortum spearheaded a drive to buy the *Balclutha* for $25,000 and restore her. More than 90 business firms and 18 Bay Area labor unions rallied to the cause, and a resplendent, "shipshape-and-Bristol-fashion" restored three-master was the result. Fifty cents admission was charged during her first year at Fisherman's Wharf and she took in $93,000. Since then the ship has earned over $6 million.

Her mainmast rises 145 feet from her deck, quickly demonstrating to the uninitiated why her kind is referred to as tall ships. The main yard, on which one of her square sails was hung, is 86 feet long. From the tip of her sturdy bowsprit to the outboard end of her spanker boom, she measures 301 feet. She weighed 1689 gross tons when she was in service, and she could carry 2660 tons of cargo. While far from a clipper in design, she could make 300 miles a day. When new, the *Balclutha* was only one of about 1500 tall ships sailing in the British merchant navy. Today she is one of fewer than a dozen of her class in the entire world. Her name comes from two Gaelic words, *baile* (town) and the native name of the Clyde River.

---

BELOW, LEFT: *The* Balclutha *prior to restoration.* BELOW, RIGHT: *The* Balclutha *under sail.* OPPOSITE: *The* Balclutha *is towed into San Francisco Bay. The Bay Bridge is in the background.*

# *Belem*

Considerably smaller than the *Balclutha* (she measures 191 feet overall and has a beam of 28 feet, 10 inches), the three-masted French bark *Belem* has led a full life. Built at Nantes in 1896, this handsome vessel, based at Le Havre, was intended for France's sugar trade to the West Indies. She brought cocoa home from South America. Between 1896 and 1913 she made 66 transatlantic passages. Her sleek lines caught the eye of England's Duke of Westminster. Rebuilt for him as a luxurious yacht, she served for a time as his home at sea. Then she was sold again, this time to A. E. Guinnes, who also used her as his yacht, taking her on a round-the-world cruise. Various changes in name were made during this period.

In 1951 the ship was acquired by Italy and converted into a sail-training ship. Twenty-eight years later, still fit and robust, the sturdy vessel was again acquired by French private interests and returned to the tricolor under her original name. Between 1980 and 1983 the *Belem* lay tied up to a wharf on the Seine, where she was used as a museum ship. The French government bought the ship in 1985 and restored her to her original glory. In addition, she was given a row of imitation gunports painted black on a white band around her hull. At the last minute it was announced that she would be sent to New York to represent France in the 1986 ceremonies honoring the centennial of the unveiling of the Statue of Liberty, which President François Mitterrand would attend, sailing on the ship at the ceremonies.

ABOVE: *The* Belem, *docked.* OPPOSITE, TOP: *The* Belem *under sail.* OPPOSITE, BOTTOM: *The* Belem *at sea, showing rigging.*

# *af Chapman*

One of the last sailing ships built of iron was the *af Chapman*. (The letters "af," not strictly part of her name, indicate that the man she is named after had a high rank in his community—something like the term "the hon.") This vessel was launched in 1888 without either an owner or a name, a small shipyard at Whitehaven, near Liverpool, having built her on speculation, even though steamers had been carrying more cargo worldwide than sail for a decade. It was recognized that the days of large sailing craft were numbered. Fortunately for the shipyard, an owner was found—Martin & Co., of Dublin, which named the new ship *Dunboyne* after a small hill near the mouth of the River Boyne, not far from Dublin. In 1988,

the *af Chapman* (the former *Dunboyne*) joined that small fraternity of historic relics of the age of sail that reached and passed the century mark.

John O'Neill, the *Dunboyne*'s first captain, had her for two decades. He and his 19-year-old bride, Kathleen O'Flaherty, had an 84-day honeymoon aboard on the trip from Antwerp to Australia. Over the following years, with her husband as midwife, she bore five children, all at sea. A depression in 1908 forced the ship to be sold and she was run until 1915 by two Norse shipping companies, which renamed her *G. D. Kennedy*. She was converted to carry boys eager to train as ship's officers. In 1924 the Swedish navy bought

her and gave the name *af Chapman,* honoring an eighteenth-century Swedish admiral. Until late 1934 the sturdy vessel sailed the globe, visiting Australasia, the Americas and Africa. Between 1937 and the end of World War II the aging ship was used as a barracks in Stockholm. In 1947 she became a youth hostel, with sleeping space for 130. Since then, more than a million guests have stayed aboard her.

She is presently one of the Swedish Touring Club's special prides, being described as the "world's most famous youth hostel." But she is more—she is one of the world's most illustrious full-rigged ships. Only two older iron ships of this kind are known to have survived—

the *Joseph Conrad* and the *Wavertree.* Her berth is in the heart of Stockholm. Some of the credit for her fine upkeep today is due to a number of the ship's former "boys," who have returned to serve her. The *af Chapman's* mainmast rises 140 feet above the deck. She is 245 feet long and has a beam of 37.5 feet. When she had sails, there were 26 of them, boasting some 24,000 square feet of canvas. The ship has been honored by being depicted on a Swedish two-kronor stamp.

---

OPPOSITE: af Chapman, *under sail.* ABOVE: af Chapman *at her Stockholm mooring.*

# Charles W. Morgan

Built in 1841, this superb whaler, named after a famous whaling merchant, is the oldest merchant ship in the United States and the last of her kind. Whalers once made up the largest and perhaps the most successful type of vessel in the American merchant marine. During her active life the ship made 37 voyages over a period of 80 years, which indicates how long each voyage was. It is said that she took more whales and sailed greater distances than any other American whaler. Her voyaging covered the globe, including the Arctic and Antarctic. The Civil War virtually destroyed the whaling fleet; Confederate raiders captured and sank many ships, but the bulk of the losses came when owners transferred ships to foreign flags to escape both the raiders and high insurance rates. The fleet was never fully restored after the war. After her retirement in 1921, the *Charles W. Morgan* spent many years at New Bedford as a museum ship. Today she is the pride of the "living museum" of Mystic Seaport, Mystic, Connecticut, and the focal point of its collection of 200 boats and ships. Restoration work has been almost continuous. For several years she was up on land, while an entirely new bottom and lower hull were built.

During her retirement from active service, the *Charles W. Morgan* has survived two major hurricanes, in 1938 and in 1954. Perhaps the most frequent comment heard as visitors leave the *Morgan* these days is how low the deck levels are. The average American today is taller than the average seaman of a century ago. Most people have to stoop when they walk through the master's quarters aboard the *Morgan.* Her length overall is 169 feet, her beam 27 feet and her depth 17 feet. The ship was built by Jethro and Zachariah Hillmann Bros., of Fairhaven, Massachusetts, and weighed 313 gross tons. When in service she had 20 sails and usually was run by a crew of 28. Her hull is of wood.

ABOVE: *The* Charles W. Morgan *at anchor at the Mystic Seaport Museum.*

# *Constellation*

Berthed at Baltimore, the U.S.F. *Constellation* is believed by many to be slightly older than the *Constitution,* having been launched in Baltimore in 1797 as the first frigate of the U.S. Navy. (Although there are some who hold that the present *Constellation* is a vessel built in 1855 by the Norfolk Navy Yard, and is actually the last sailing warship built by the Navy, during her present restoration nails bearing the date stamps 1797, 1808 and 1812 were found.) During World War II President Franklin D. Roosevelt designated her flagship of the Atlantic Fleet, her last command.

The U.S.F. *Constellation* Foundation, present owner of the ship, has every reason to be proud of the ship and of its work. A large crew of volunteers, under the guidance of Commander Thomas K. Boots, is helping in restoring the ship. For the restoration of the ship's quarter deck, it took over three years to obtain a kind of wood that met specifications—a dense grade of Douglas fir was required and had to be brought by truck from the West Coast. Of the first 8000 feet acquired, 6000 had to be rejected. Each of the new deck beams measured 14″ × 14″ × 38″, weighed about half a ton and cost $3000. The *Constellation* is 259 feet in length, 42 feet wide and has a draft of 20 feet. Her displacement tonnage is 1960 tons. Many years of work remain before she will be fully restored.

ABOVE, TOP: *Spar-deck restoration on the* Constellation, *1988.*
ABOVE, BOTTOM: *The* Constellation *docked at the Inner Harbor, Baltimore.*

# Constitution

Better known to the world as "Old Ironsides," the U.S.S. *Constitution* is the oldest commissioned ship in the U.S. Navy. A full-rigged ship with an overall length of 305 feet, a beam of 43.5 feet and a draft of 19.8 feet, she was built at the Edmond Hartt Shipyard in Boston and launched in 1797. A highlight of her career came during the War of 1812, when she was victorious over the British ship *Guerrière,* which had been seized by the British from the French. (During the battle, the steering wheel of the American warship was destroyed. After the surrender of the *Guerrière,* her steering wheel was taken off and put in position on the *Constitution.* Years later it was presented to the American Merchant Marine Museum, where I am curator.)

The nickname "Old Ironsides" was given the ship when British cannonballs bounced off the oak planking of the American frigate's hull. During the conflict the *Constitution* was undefeated in 40 engagements. After her service in the War of 1812 and exploits against the pirates of Tripoli and Algiers, the ship was badly neglected. She was about to be scrapped in 1830 when Oliver Wendell Holmes, a 21-year-old son of a minister, came to her defense with a poem, "Old Ironsides." It so caught the imagination of its readers that there was a deluge of protests against the scrapping. The ship has retained her commission in the Navy ever since.

Today the *Constitution* is towed away from her Boston berth to be turned around twice a year "so that her timbers will wear evenly." In 1932 the ship made a tour of Atlantic, Gulf and West Coast ports. I would like to see her reequipped with sails and sailors and sent on another similar tour so that every schoolchild in America might have a chance to board her.

BELOW: *The* Constitution *in a view taken at New Orleans during Carnival, 1932.*

# Cutty Sark

The noted British author Basil Lubbock, in the preface of his famous book *The Log of the Cutty Sark* (1924), says of this illustrious British clipper: "Next to the *Victory,* the most interesting survivor of the days of sail is undoubtedly the famous tea and wool clipper, *Cutty Sark.*" Enshrined at this writing in her dry dock at the National Maritime Museum, Greenwich, England, the wonderful craft is seen by many thousands each year. She was built at Dumbarton on the Clyde and was launched November 23, 1869.

Harold A. Underhill, in his classic work *Sail Training and Cadet Ships,* explains how she was constructed with a most generous use of teak. He wrote: "The story told locally is that every foot of timber which went into her was examined . . . and rejected for the smallest superficial blemish even though the timber was perfectly sound. Labor and wastage exceeded the estimate by a large margin."

So much so, Underhill added, that the builders went into liquidation. Her life, however, was a long and useful one. At the end of the nineteenth century, when speed was no longer essential in sailing ships, the *Cutty Sark* was sold to a Portuguese firm owned by J. A. Ferreira. Renamed *Ferreira,* she became a tramp, carrying pig iron, lumber and such cargoes until 1916. In 1922 she was sold again and once again renamed, becoming the *Maria de Amparo.* Saved for posterity by a Capt. W. H. Dowman, she got her original name back and was brought home to England. After surviving a number of difficult years she was eventually turned over to the museum at Greenwich. She is the world's last surviving true clipper ship.

BELOW: *The* Cutty Sark.

# *Dar Pomorza*

This gallant vessel, built in 1909 in Germany, was first named the *Prinzess Eitel Friedrich*. She was turned over to the French after World War I and renamed *Colbert*. In 1929 the ship was bought by the people of Poland, and given to the Polish state as a training ship for merchant marine officers. She was renamed *Dar Pomorza* ("The Gift of Pomorze") a name she has retained. In 1972 she was the first ship from behind the Iron Curtain to join Britain's Sail Training Association ship races. The *Dar Pomorza* came to New York in 1976 to participate in the Bicentennial OpSail accompanied by a fleet of small Polish sail-training vessels. After 1976 the 298-foot-long ship was retired. She remains in Gdynia as a museum ship.

BELOW, LEFT AND RIGHT: *The* Dar Pomorza.

# *Elissa*

The *Elissa* was constructed of iron in a shipyard in Aberdeen, Scotland, in 1877. Her home port at this writing is Galveston, and she is owned by the Galveston Historical Foundation. Originally she sailed under the British flag, but she was sold to Norway in 1897, to Sweden in 1911 and to Finland in 1930. Only 145.5 feet long on deck, she has an overall length of 202 feet, including her spars. Her beam is 28 feet and she has a depth of 16 feet. The *Elissa*'s mainmast rises 102 feet above the deck. As rebuilt at Galveston, she has 19 sails with 12,000 feet of canvas. Her gross tonnage is 430 tons; she carries 245 tons of ballast. The ship's small size probably extended the length of her active life, as she could be used on routes where her shallow draft permitted her to sail.

Before the *Elissa* was discovered by Karl Kortum and others she was being used by Greek operators as a motor-powered cargo ship.

After being alerted by Kortum, a group of historically minded Texans bought the hulk in 1975. She had visited Galveston in 1883 and in 1886, justifying their interest. The ship's slow progress from Greece to Gibraltar to Galveston is a tribute to the determination of those who saved her. She finally arrived in 1979. Then began the even harder assignment of raising the substantial funds needed to restore her. The goal that made the difficult fund-raising possible was the hope that she could come to New York on July 4, 1986, for OpSail. And she made it! She was in the parade, shining and restored to a peak of perfection and manned by an outstanding group of young people.

ABOVE: *The* Elissa *under sail.* OVERLEAF: *The* Elissa's *crew at work.*

ABOVE: *The* Elissa.

# Falls of Clyde

Pride of the Hawaii Maritime Center in Honolulu, the *Falls of Clyde* is the last full-rigged, four-masted sailing ship in the world, another of the tall ships saved with the help of Karl Kortum. Not only is this ship the only vessel boasting square sails on four masts, but she is one of the few remaining ships built of iron instead of steel. (Iron lasts much longer in salt water, and the ship's preservation has been helped considerably by her iron hull. Ships with steel hulls rust quicker and require frequent costly dry-dockings.) The *Falls of Clyde* was built in 1878 at Port Glasgow, Scotland. The ship's length is 266 feet. Her beam is 40 feet and she has a depth of 23.5 feet. Her gross tonnage measurement is 1807 tons.

The ship's long career began with many years in worldwide trade, followed by 21 years as a sailing oil tanker for the Matson Navigation Co., bringing oil from the mainland to Hawaii and returning with molasses. New owners took her to Ketchikan, Alaska, where she was used for years as an oil depot ship—afloat but never sailing. In 1958 she was moved to Seattle by a new owner who hoped to open her as a museum ship, but the plan failed for lack of funds.

In 1963 it was decided to sink her as a breakwater in Vancouver, British Columbia. Meanwhile, a mounting campaign to save the historic ship had been started in Hawaii, where her long career under the Matson house flag had made her famous. At the last moment $18,000 was raised and the ship was acquired by a group of Hawaiian citizens. With the help of the U.S. Navy the ship was towed to Honolulu. After various adventures, including weathering Hurricane Iwa, the *Falls of Clyde* came to have a permanent berth at Honolulu's Pier 7, alongside the famous Kalakaua Boathouse.

ABOVE: *The* Falls of Clyde *at berth in Honolulu.* OVERLEAF, TOP: *The captain's salon aboard the* Falls of Clyde. OVERLEAF, BOTTOM: *The* Falls of Clyde *under sail.*

ABOVE: *The* Falls of Clyde.

# *Gazela Primeiro*

This was the oldest tall ship of the Class A variety (ships of 150 feet in length or over) in Operation Sail 1976 in New York. She was built of wood at Cacilhas, Portugal, in 1883, the timbers used coming from a national forest planted in 1460 by Prince Henry the Navigator. The *Gazela Primeiro* is 186.6 feet long, has a beam of 27 feet and a sail area of 8910 square feet. She operated out of the Canary Islands, under the Portuguese flag, fishing off the Grand Banks for her long commercial life, which included some whaling, as evidenced by the discovery, years later, of two old harpoons in one of her lockers. The old vessel was bought for the Philadelphia Maritime Museum by one of its benefactors, the late William Smith, and was sailed to Philadelphia in time to be a part of the Bicentennial.

A sturdy but somewhat makeshift crew headed by a brave tugboat captain made it possible for this ancient craft to sail to Bermuda to start out with the largest collection of tall ships ever assembled in the world in this century for New York and OpSail 1976. There was such a crush of vessels crossing the starting line that several minor collisions took place. One was between the *Gazela* and the huge Spanish four-master *Juan Sebastián de Elcano*.

The old former fishing schooner lost her main topmast and much rigging. While the *Gazela* was limping to Newport, it was found that Mystic Seaport had her sail plan, as well as a specialist in masts and rigging. Best of all, they had a seasoned piece of North Carolina timber just right for a new topmast. By the time the *Gazela* got to Newport, the new topmast had been cut, trimmed, shaped, finished and loaded on the roof of a truck and taken to the Rhode Island port. Three days later the *Gazela Primeiro* sailed into New York harbor with new rigging and a new main topmast—right on schedule and in her appointed place in line. It was worth all the effort. An estimated seven million people lined the harbor to watch OpSail 1976. In the years that followed that colorful event, the old former Portuguese fishing vessel was renamed *Gazela of Philadelphia*. She participated in the 1986 Operation Sail in New York and has been a part of several other great sail gatherings. Berthed at Penn's Landing, Philadelphia, she is being used as a training ship by the Philadelphia Ship Preservation Guild. She can accommodate a crew of 20 with 32 cadets.

ABOVE: *The* Gazela Primeiro.

# James Craig

The *James Craig* was the first of the famous Clan Line of sailing ships owned by Thomas Dunlop. She was built at Sunderland, England, in 1874, beginning life as the *Clan Macleod*. A three-masted bark, she was 180 feet in length with a beam of 31 feet. While voyaging as a tramp cargo carrier, the smart little ship had a young Australian sailor aboard who became one of the world's best-known writers about tall ships—Alan Villiers. In his book *The Set of the Sails* he had this to say about her: "The *James Craig* was a lovely little vessel. There was a graceful rake to her high masts, and a lovely line to her sheer which spoke of sea kindliness. I had not been with her very long, but I felt that as long as I lived I would owe her something. Something of me would be with her as long as she survived." Despite adversities, the *James Craig* has survived.

After sailing for half a century, she was abandoned in a bay in Tasmania, where she lay neglected and almost forgotten for 40 years. Photographs taken of her there show no masts, only a stub of a bowsprit, but a hull virtually intact. Thanks to the Sydney Maritime Museum and some help from the Australian National Industries, the *James Craig* is now on display, partially restored, in Darling Harbor, Sydney. The deck is ready for fund-raising parties. David M. Hill, the project manager for the restoration, has summarized the importance of the restoration as "making an important contribution to our knowledge and understanding of maritime life, ship construction and operation, and the impact of the sea and shipping on Australian development and everyday life in the 19th Century."

BELOW: *The partially restored* James Craig *on display in Darling Harbour, Sydney, 1988.* OPPOSITE, TOP: *The* James Craig *in New York harbor, 1890s.* OPPOSITE, BOTTOM: *The* James Craig *undergoing restoration, 1986.*

# Joseph Conrad

In 1880, Georg Stage, the only son of wealth Danish shipowner Frederik Stage, died. In 1882, to create a practical memorial to the boy, Stage funded the construction of a small training ship, the *Georg Stage,* accommodating 80 boys on a cruise program lasting five months each year. The plan, still in operation, began with a group of young men selected annually. Training started with a three-week period of drill followed by a series of one-day trips and then by longer cruises.

The vessel operated without accident for her first 25 years, but in 1905, she was hit by another ship and sank with the loss of 22. The fund paid for raising her and rebuilding her with proper watertight compartments and she operated until 1922, when she had another major refit. In 1934, just as the ship was to be sold for scrap and replaced by a new vessel of the same name, Alan Villiers, the noted author, saw her, fell in love with her and bought her. He renamed her the *Joseph Conrad,* and installed a new figurehead portraying the famous author. For the next three years she flew the British flag, logging 57,800 miles with Villiers at the helm.

In 1936 Villiers sold her to the wealthy American food merchant Huntington Hartford, who rebuilt her as his private yacht, installing a small diesel engine in the process. When war came, Hartford gave her to the United States to use as a training ship, a duty she performed until 1947. At that point the government turned her over to Mystic Seaport to help train Sea Scouts and Girl Mariners. She remains one of the star attractions at Mystic. The *Joseph Conrad* is a full-rigged ship: She has square sails on all three masts. Built of iron, the *Joseph Conrad* has a gross of 203 tons, a length of 118 feet, a beam of 25 feet and a draft of 11 feet.

ABOVE AND OPPOSITE: *The* Joseph Conrad.

# *Mayflower II*

Author-skipper Alan Villiers brought this reconstruction of the Pilgrim ship *Mayflower* to New York in 1956. It was not easy to build a reconstruction of a ship of which there are no plans or contemporary pictures. The *Mayflower* was already old in 1620, when the Pilgrims chartered her to bring their band of 103 to North America. A comparison of ships of her day having the same tonnage suggests that the *Mayflower* may have been between 52 and 73 feet along her keel, with a breadth of perhaps 24 to 27 feet and a depth of from 10 to 13 feet. There is a possibility that her wood was used to build a barn that is still standing in Buckingham-

shire, England. The reconstruction was built in Brixham, Devon, by Stuart Upham. There were 33 in her crew on the Atlantic trip. Alan Villiers took 53 days to make it, while the original ship had taken 67 days. The ship measures 183 tons, a little more than the original *Mayflower*. With frequent maintenance work done on her, she has survived the past 35 years and remains a central feature of Plimoth Plantation, Plymouth, Massachusetts.

---

ABOVE AND OPPOSITE: *The* Mayflower.

# *Passat*

The *Passat* was built in 1911 at Blohm & Voss's great Hamburg shipyard for the famous "P" Line, all of whose ships had names beginning with the letter "P." Her identical sister ship, built the same year, was the *Peking*. According to a story, the bride of the shipowner F. Laeisz owned a poodle. In a moment of affection he promised that all the ships in his fleet would have names starting with "P" to honor the poodle, and that a figure of a poodle would be the company's symbol. Other notable ships of his fleet were the *Pamir, Padua, Peking* and *Pommern.*

The *Passat* (the name means "tradewind") survived two serious collisions while she was under the Laeisz house flag. After World War I she was owned briefly by the French, but was bought back by Laeisz and returned to the German flag. In 1932 Gustaf Erikson, of Mariehamn, Finland, acquired her. A notable figure in sailing-ship circles, this famous shipowner retained the names of the various tall ships he bought, running them on the grain trade from Australia to Europe. Even after World War II the *Passat* and the *Pamir* were run briefly by the Erikson company on the same grain route. Sold to ship breakers, the *Passat* was saved and became a cadet-training ship. The *Pamir* was lost with many deaths in 1957. At this point the *Passat,* owned by the city of Lübeck, became a dormitory for young people. She was tied up at Travemünde, on the Baltic.

---

ABOVE: *Work on one of the* Passat's *masts.* OPPOSITE, TOP: *The* Passat *under sail.* OPPOSITE, MIDDLE: *The* Passat *at Travemünde.* OPPOSITE, BOTTOM: *The* Passat *encounters rough seas.*

# *Peking*

Built in 1911 by Blohm & Voss, Hamburg, the *Peking* was another of the famous Laeisz Line of huge steel windjammers that bravely made the last stand of sail in the pre–World War II era. Of 3100 gross tons, she had an extreme length of 377.5 feet and an extreme beam of 47 feet. Retired from the sea in 1932, she served as an English boys' school under the name *Arethusa.* In 1975, one of the South Street Seaport Museum's staunchest supporters, Jack Aron, took it upon himself to fly to England and buy the *Peking* for the seaport museum, where, berthed at Pier 16, she is the largest ship in the museum's fleet. Although restoration will be slow work, it has started, and visitors to the museum can see her as she was in action in a film made by a young American seaman, Irving Johnson, during one of her trips around Cape Horn.

ABOVE: *The* Peking *under sail.* OPPOSITE: *The* Peking *at anchor at South Street Seaport, New York.*

*Polly Woodside*
*May 1977*

# *Polly Woodside*

The *Polly Woodside* was the product of Workman Clark & Co., a noted Belfast shipbuilder. When new in 1885 she was quite ordinary—just one of tens of thousands of similar ships. She had nice lines, but there was nothing about her that might lead people to believe she would survive for over a century and be recognized as a priceless nautical artifact. The ship had only one forward (or collision) bulkhead and would have sunk abruptly had she been holed anywhere but at her stem. (Many other ships did just that.) The lives of seamen were not valued very highly and safety regulations were virtually unknown. She was of iron, of course, and was bark-rigged. Having square sails on her fore- and mainmasts and fore-and-aft sails on the mizzen permitted her owners to use a smaller crew (only 15) than would have been required on a full-rigged ship. She was 230 feet overall, had a beam of 30 feet and a draft of only 14 feet. Her gross tonnage was only 678, and her original owner was the William J. Woodside Co. Her sail area was 11,000 square feet and her maximum speed was a respectable 14 knots. She could carry 1100 tons of cargo. Her mainmast rose 108 feet above the deck and her main yard was 65 feet long.

In her first 19 years, the *Polly Woodside* lost only four men. In 1904 she was sold to a New Zealand owner, who renamed her *Rona*. Her sailing days came to an end shortly after the end of World War I and she was dismantled for use as a lighter. Somehow she survived, and during World War II was towed to New Guinea as part of a fleet of hulks supplying the armed forces. Towed back to Australia when peace came, the *Polly Woodside* worked as a coal barge in Melbourne. In 1968 her owners donated her to the National Trust of Australia. By that time she had become the last sailing ship afloat in all of that island continent. Karl Kortum brought her to the attention of Australian preservationists and in 1972 some volunteers began cleaning her up. Two years later, a dry-docking showed that her iron hull was in good shape. By 1978 she was moved to a permanent berth in Dukes & Orr's Dock, Melbourne, and opened to visitors. In 1988 the World Ship Trust of London awarded the Melbourne Maritime Museum its Heritage Award for its achievement in preserving the *Polly Woodside*.

ABOVE: *The* Polly Woodside *undergoing restoration, 1977.* OPPOSITE: *The restored* Polly Woodside, *Melbourne.*

# *Pommern*

The *Pommern* was built in 1903 by J. Reid & Co., Ltd., of Greenock, Scotland, for B. Wencke & Sons, of Hamburg. Originally named *Mneme* (Greek for "memory"), she boasted a Greek goddess as a figurehead. As fate would have it, the Greeks did own her briefly. She received her present name in 1906, when she was added to Laeisz' "P" Line fleet. Her gross was 2376 tons. She had an overall length of 349 feet and an extreme beam of 43 feet. Her draft was 21 feet. Her mainmast rose 152 feet above the deck. Its mainyard was 91 feet long. She had no auxiliary engine, but was equipped with 27 sails. In 1921 the big vessel was turned over to Greece as a war reparation. She failed to pay off and Gustaf Erikson, of Mariehamn, Finland, bought her, working her until war began again. In 1952

Erikson gave her to the town of Mariehamn. In 1989 the *Pommern* was given a new deck which cost 1.6 million Finnish marks.

The *Pommern* is one of the few museum ships that have left their regular berths and made trips under tow to maritime functions held elsewhere. In 1987 she was towed to Stockholm. A number of other proposals to charter the great vessel and tow, or even sail her, have been received. To move her under her own sail, however, would be extremely expensive.

---

ABOVE: *The* Pommern. OPPOSITE, TOP: *The* Pommern's *figurehead.* OPPOSITE, BOTTOM: *The* Pommern *under sail.*

# *Sigyn*

Eight different shipowners owned this little wooden bark for her first half-century but she has been the property of a single owner for her second 50 years. The *Sigyn* slid down the ways on July 15, 1887, in the port city of Göteborg, Sweden. She is the last wooden bark of her type in the world. Made of oak and pine, her hull was copper-sheathed up to the load waterline, the copper being secured to the hull by both wooden and copper bolts. From the start this craft was greatly admired for her lovely lines and the fine proportions of her rigging. She and her sister ship, the *Gurli,* were often called "Hübe's beauties," in reference to their builder, J. H. Hübe.

The *Sigyn* is 378 gross tons, 180 feet in overall length, 30.6 feet in beam and 13 feet draft. With her original bark rig she had a sail area of 8611 square feet, and used 20 sails. Later, as a barkentine, she had 16 sails. She usually had a crew of ten plus her master. She sailed to Canada, the United States, the Caribbean, ports in South America, North Africa, South Africa, the Canary Islands and Bangkok. A fine sailer, she could make 13 knots with the wind on her quarter and

seven when tacking. Among her best voyages was one of 34 days from Liverpool to Puerto Rico. Her best single day's run may have been the time she did 276.5 nautical miles, averaging over 11 knots.

In 1913, she was driven ashore near Kristiansand, Norway, and was seriously damaged and condemned. But salvage experts refloated her and she was towed to Sweden and repaired. Her life had only begun. Her last commercial voyage ended in 1937 and the next year the Maritime Museum at Turku, Finland, bought her. She was out on display in 1939. Bomb splinters inflicted some damage during World War II, but despite shortages of material and money, the museum maintained the ship. In 1954 a film assignment saw her set sail for a few hours off Turku. In 1971 and 1975 dry-docking strengthened her hull, which had begun to hog (arch along her keel). In 1979 she was rerigged. A tour aboard her reveals the primitive conditions under which seamen of her day served.

ABOVE: *The* Sigyn *under sail.* OPPOSITE: *The* Sigyn *after restoration, at Turku.*

# Star of India

There are good reasons for ranking the *Star of India* as America's most distinguished bark: Not only is she older than all other museum sailing cargo ships in America (exceeded in age only by the whaler *Charles W. Morgan*), but she is built of iron and is still able to sail. Were it not for overwhelmingly high insurance costs, the *Star of India* could be sailing much of the year. Instead she has been forced to limit herself to a few short afternoon excursions out of her pier at San Diego. As Craig Arnold, editor of the Maritime Museum Association of San Diego's house magazine, *Mains'l Haul,* put it: "*Star of India* is a private time capsule—one that transports us back to the glorious Age of Sail, the time of clippers, East Indiamen, proud frigates and a host of others."

This superb three-master, built as a full-rigged ship, was launched on November 14, 1863, by Gibson, McDonald & Arnold, at Ramsey, Isle of Man, under the name *Euterpe* (the Muse of Music). Her first owners were Wakefield, Nash & Co., Liverpool. On each of her first two trips to Calcutta, she suffered bad weather and was involved in a collision. On her second return passage her captain died. Losing money, the owners sold the ship; eventually she was operated by Shaw, Savill & Albion, one of Britain's most famous shipping enterprises. The vessel remained with the company for 27 years, sailing from England to South Australia and New Zealand, frequently returning via the Pacific Coast. Captain T. E. Phillips made ten successive trips around the world aboard her. The *Euterpe* often carried emigrants. In 1901 she was bought by the Alaska Packers' Association, which had a fleet of tall ships, all with names starting with the word "Star." She became the *Star of India* and was converted into a bark. Her poop was extended almost to the mainmast and the forward deckhouse was widened. On this run the ship often carried as many as 200 seamen, fishermen and cannery workers.

In 1926 the vessel was bought by the Zoological Society of San Diego, but the project they had planned came to naught because of the Depression. Men like author Jerry MacMullen and Kenneth Reynard organized a fund to restore her. Their success, and the work done by countless others since, have given San Diego the prize of all museum ships—a working square-rigger.

BELOW AND OPPOSITE: *The* Star of India.

# *Suomen Joutsen*

A large and handsome ship, the *Suomen Joutsen* was built in 1902. Launched as the *Laënnec* for the Société des Armateurs Nantais, she carried nitrates and other cargo. Then H. H. Schmidt bought her and changed her name to *Oldenburg*. She continued in the nitrate trade but also carried young men training to become merchant-marine officers in the German cargo-ship fleet. Sold once again, she became a training ship for the North German Lloyd, the great German liner company based in Bremerhaven. The NGL needed a continuous supply of young officers for their fleet of passenger ships operating on worldwide routes. In 1931 the government of Finland bought the ship and gave her her present name, which means "swan of Finland."

Despite a number of accidents, this lovely ship is one of the finest examples of the large full-rigged sailing ship built of steel still in existence. She lies at Turku, the old capital of Finland. Although her active days as a training ship are past, Turku would not part with her. Her lines are so perfect that, at first impression, she seems smaller than she really is. When I walked around her decks and interior spaces in February 1990, I was amazed at how large she in fact is: The ship has a gross of 2260 tons, with an overall length of 315 feet and an extreme beam of 40 feet. She has a draft of 17 feet. The ship originally had 27 sails and a sail area of 24,220 square feet. Her mainmast rises 170 feet above the waterline. When used for training she had space for 150 cadets. In her later life diesel engines with 2200 horsepower were installed that could give her a speed of six knots under power alone. The *Suomen Joutsen* has wooden decks but her hull, deck houses and masts are steel.

ABOVE: *The* Suomen Joutsen *at Turku.*

# Susan Constant, Godspeed and Discovery

In 1957 the Jamestown Festival, Virginia, was held to commemorate the three-hundred-fiftieth anniversary of the founding of America's first permanent English settlement. Three ship reconstructions were built for this event and sailed over from England. They were the *Susan Constant, Godspeed* and *Discovery*. The originals had landed in America on April 26, 1607, bearing colonists who named the river they found the James and their community Jamestown. About 105 settlers and three crews totaling 39 had made the trip, coming over under the sponsorship of the London Company. The ships were tiny by today's standards: The *Susan Constant* was 120 tons; the *Godspeed* measured 40 tons and the *Discovery* was only 20 tons. The trio of replicas was designed by Robert G. C. Fee, a naval architect associated with the Newport News Shipbuilding & Dry Dock Co., Newport News, Virginia, who had built a model of the *Susan Constant* in the 1940s. The ships were built in West Norfolk, near Portsmouth, England, by Curtis-Dunn Marine Industries, Ltd. Although very little is known of what the original ships looked like, the design followed a painting of the three by Commander Griffith Bailey Coale. Both Fee and Coale had done extensive research.

The three replicas were popular attractions at the Jamestown Settlement park. For many years only the *Susan Constant* was open to the public. Weather and general deterioration made replacements vital. New replicas of the *Godspeed* and the *Discovery* were built in the early 1980s. They can actually be sailed and this has been done on a number of occasions. The *Godspeed,* in fact, was sent to England aboard a modern cargo ship in 1985 to reenact the 1607 voyage. She followed the route taken by the original settlers from London to the Canary Islands, across the Atlantic to the Caribbean and then north to Virginia. The *Godspeed* also participated in the 1986 OpSail gathering in New York harbor. A new *Susan Constant* has just been built. This view shows the original *Susan Constant* reconstruction and the replacements of the two smaller vessels. Stanley Potter, of Beaufort, North Carolina, was the naval architect for the new *Susan Constant* replica. Much of his work was based on new research done by British marine historian Brian Lavery.

BELOW: *The* Susan Constant *(left), the* Godspeed *(middle) and the* Discovery *(right) at Jamestown.* OVERLEAF, TOP: *A plan of the* Susan Constant. OVERLEAF, BOTTOM: *The* Godspeed *under sail.*

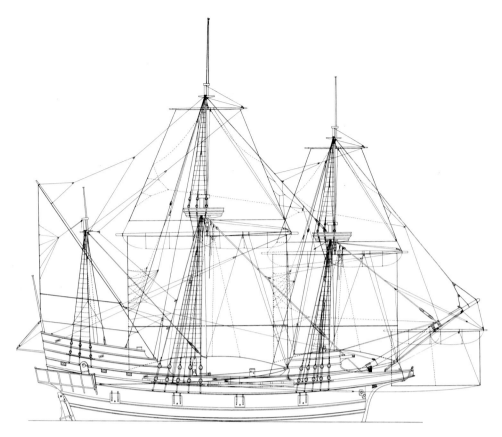

ABOVE: *The* Susan Constant *and the* Godspeed.

# Vasa

Built in 1627, the *Vasa* was the largest Swedish warship of that day and one of the world's greatest—length: 230 feet; extreme beam: 38 feet; draft (aft): 16 feet. Her mainmast rose 160 feet above the keel and she was of 1300 tons displacement. Ordered by King Gustav II Adolf of Sweden, she was built by the Royal Naval Shipyard, Stockholm. But her fatal flaw was her armament of 64 guns; the King had ordered an extra gun deck without any knowledge of what it would do to the ship's stability in the water. On her maiden voyage, with many visitors aboard, the gallant ship turned over at the first blow of wind from the north and went down. She lay covered by silt in Stockholm harbor until, in the face of widespread skepticism, Anders Franzen located the wreck in 1956, after a two-year search.

Once the *Vasa* was identified, the salvage was taken under royal patronage, insuring the finest engineering technology. She was raised in 1961 and housed in a museum designed to hold her. Today she is the greatest tourist attraction in Scandinavia, and one of the most remarkable nautical artifacts preserved in the world. In July 1990 a second, larger and more extraordinary *Vasa* Museum was opened in Stockholm, featuring seven different viewing levels and a full-size replica of half the main deck, with the ship's lower masts restored and in place and her lower yards and rigging visible. The *Vasa* affords us a glimpse of life in 1628, for in the wreck were thousands upon thousands of artifacts such as clothing, carvings, utensils, arms—even drinkable beer and edible cheese. All had been preserved in nature's own icebox under layers of cold, wet clay.

BELOW: *Upper deck of the* Vasa. OVERLEAF, TOP: *The* Vasa *being transported in Stockholm harbor.* OVERLEAF, BOTTOM: *The* Vasa, *with open gunports.*

ABOVE: *The* Vasa.

# *Victory*

Linking the period of history between the *Vasa* and "Old Ironsides" is the British Navy's historic ship-of-the-line *Victory,* on which Horatio Nelson lost his life while defeating Napoleon's fleet at the Battle of Trafalgar, October 21, 1805. The proportions of the job of building this ship, designed by Sir Thomas Slade, may be seen in the time it took to complete her. The keel was laid in 1759 but was not launched until six years laters, and the ship was not commissioned until 15 years after that, perhaps due to politics.

The great ship was constructed at the Chatham Dockyard, Chatham, Kent. Her mainmast rises 203 feet above the waterline, higher even than that of any ocean liner ever built except the Italian superliner *Rex.* Her length overall was 328 feet, with a hull length of 226 feet. Her extreme beam was 52 feet and the draft was 19 feet, eight inches. At Trafalgar she had a complement of 850 officers, men and marines and carried 104 guns, although intended as a 100-gun ship. There were three principal gun decks, as opposed to two on the *Constitution.* She had a 3500-ton displacement. The preservation of this extraordinary ship, still owned by the Royal Navy, as a museum vessel at Portsmouth Naval Dockyard is of major importance.

I was in Portsmouth in 1974 rounding up tall ships to come to New York for the Bicentennial in 1976. I saw the *Victory* there and then watched Prince Philip (Chairman of the British Sail Training Association) review a large fleet of square-rigged sail-training ships from all over the globe.

ABOVE AND OVERLEAF: *The* Victory.

ABOVE: *The* Victory

# *Viking*

Here is another of the great four-masted barks that are queens of today's museum ships. The world owes a debt of gratitude to Gustaf Erikson for preserving the *Viking* well after sail had been abandoned by almost everyone else. Built in 1907 by Burmeister & Wain, Copenhagen, this handsome tall ship was designed as a merchant-marine training vessel for A/S Den Danske Handelsflaades Skoleskib for Befalingsmaend, of Denmark. She was built to accommodate up to 150 trainees, as well as a crew of 32. Before she was completed, a gust of wind tipped her over at the fitting-out berth; she had no ballast aboard. Fortunately, the ship fell over toward the pier and did not sink, only slightly delaying her delivery. The cadets aboard were housed by extending the ship's poop to include the Liverpool house amidships, giving a 200-foot-long deckhouse. The 2959-gross-ton ship has kept the name *Viking* throughout her career—something unusual for a great sailing ship of this period. A length of 240 feet overall made her one of the largest tall ships ever built. Her extreme beam is 45 feet, seven inches. Her draft is 23 feet. The *Viking*'s mast rises 154 feet above her deck. The ship's 31 sails have a total area of 30,680 square feet.

The great size of the *Viking* made her a difficult vessel to operate profitably. Before World War I she sailed in the nitrate trade between Hamburg and Peru, then she was sold to Det Forenede Dampskibsselskab and kept in service until 1925, when she was laid up until she was bought for the Australian grain trade by Gustaf Erikson of Mariehamn. During World War II she was used as a grain-storage ship. One final voyage under the management of an aging Erikson took place in 1946 when, with a crew of 32, she took timber to South Africa and returned with 4000 tons of grain. After Erikson's death the great ship was laid up again. In 1949 the City of Göteborg, Sweden, bought her to use as a stationary training ship for seamen. Two years later she was towed there from Antwerp with 2000 tons of coke. Her arrival was the cause of a gala harbor ceremony. For the past four decades, the *Viking* has been well maintained by Göteborg.

ABOVE, RIGHT AND OVERLEAF: *The* Viking.

# *Wavertree*

The *Wavertree* was built in Southampton, England in 1885 as the *Southgate.* She sailed for many years with cargoes of grain and nitrates, using many different routes worldwide. I was Program Director at the South Street Seaport Museum during the acquisition of the *Wavertree,* then the largest iron sailing ship in the world and laid up in Argentina. Peter Stanford, founder of the Seaport, was helped in this endeavor by Karl Kortum. Eventually we got her, but we could not afford to pay for a tow to bring the 293-foot, 2700-gross-ton ship up from Argentina. In 1968, the Argentine training ship *Libertad* arrived with a small piece of the *Wavertree*'s mainmast aboard. In 1970 the vessel herself was brought up by a Dutch tug that had chanced to end up a tow at the Argentine capital city. In 1976, for the Bicentennial, the Göteborg Museum had decided to give South Street the *Southgate*'s original bell, which had been in its collection. It was delivered during the celebrations in an admiral's barge, an admiral sitting in the stern, the bell on his lap. Over the years since, the *Wavertree* has been slowly and carefully restored under Jacob Isbrandtsen and his team of volunteers.

ABOVE: *The* Wavertree *in an antique photograph.* LEFT: *The* Wavertree *is painted.* OVERLEAF: *A winter view of the* Wavertree *at the South Street Seaport Museum. To the left is the* Peking.

ABOVE: *The* Wavertree.

# National Ships

# *Amerigo Vespucci*

The *Amerigo Vespucci* and her sister ship *Cristoforo Colombo* were built in 1931 at Castellammare di Stabia, Italy, by the Italian Royal Shipyard. (The *Colombo* was seized after World War II by the Soviets and renamed the *Dunay*.) Both ships are of the old style, looking more like Nelson's *Victory* than any modern sail-training craft. These huge ships have black hulls with two white stripes dotted with large ports that were meant to look like gun openings. The *Vespucci*'s length is 331.6 feet, overall. Her beam is 50 feet, ten inches and her draft is 21.6 feet. Her mainmast rises 151 feet over the deck, while her 23 sails have a 22,600-square-foot area. Many features are of the old style, from her ten-knot speed to her staff of 40 servants to serve her 150 cadets. The ship's bow and stern decorations are intricate and gilded. She has a lifesize figurehead of

Amerigo Vespucci himself. The wardrooms are elegant in decoration. In addition to regular participation in the Sail Training Association's tall-ship trips along the coast of Europe every two years, this colorful vessel came to America in 1976 and 1986 for two OpSails. She is particularly remembered because each time she has entered New York harbor her cadets have stood at attention on the ratlines all the way between the Verrazano Bridge and the George Washington Bridge, a 20-mile route.

---

ABOVE: *The* Amerigo Vespucci *under sail.* OPPOSITE, TOP: *The* Amerigo Vespucci *at the Bicentennial Operation Sail, 1976.* OPPOSITE, BOTTOM: *The* Amerigo Vespucci *in a view of 1951.*

# Capitán Miranda

An oddball ship if there ever was one, reflecting many changes in design over a 60-year career, the *Capitán Miranda* was Uruguay's representative at the 1986 OpSail in New York. Few ships have been put to so many different uses, each requiring substantial rebuilding. She was launched in Cádiz, Spain, in 1930, by the Factoría de Matagorda shipyard as a sail-powered cargo ship. After World War II she was rebuilt without sails and run as a clipper-bowed, power-driven craft—an anachronism for the period. In the 1960s her sturdy hull was again rebuilt to make her a hydrographic survey ship for the Uruguayan Navy.

In 1978 the craft was again taken in hand and rebuilt as a naval training ship. This time she emerged, renamed in honor of Captain Francisco P. Miranda, as a three-masted staysail schooner, with a gawky two-deck-high bridge between the fore and mainmasts and an implausible promenade deck stretching aft for much of the ship's length. All this top hamper gives her the look of a ship that is entirely too low in the water. The ship's portholes in the deck below the two-deck superstructure seem as though they could not help but be continually awash. Sitting on the deck amidships would put you so close to the water that your toes could easily touch the waves if you were so inclined. A good wind would heel the ship over to such an extent that green water might well wash the decks from the mainmast aft. Nevertheless, the ship has apparently had an accident-free life and performs well. One reason she appears to have such a low freeboard may be the large white band painted on her hull from the bowsprit all the way aft. Amidships its lower edge is almost at waterline. The dimensions of the *Capitán Miranda* make her one of the world's major sailing ships. She is 205 feet long, overall, and has a beam of 26 feet, three inches with a draft of 11 feet. A diesel engine permits her a maximum speed under power of eight knots. The ship weighs 715 gross tons and has a crew of 82, including from 31 to 40 cadets. She is schooner-rigged, with fore-and-aft sails only. Her homeport is Montevideo.

ABOVE: *The* Capitán Miranda.

# *Christian Radich*

The *Christian Radich* is, perhaps, the best-known tall ship in the world. She has had an eventful life since she was built in Norway in 1937 for the Kristiania Schoolship Association to train sailors for the merchant marine. Named after her patron, who commissioned her as a sail-training ship, her home port was soon transferred to Oslo. Most of her life she has been owned by the Ostlandets Skoleskib (a schoolship association) of that port, not by the Norwegian Navy. Built by Framnaes mek. Verksted, of Sandefjord, she replaced an earlier vessel, the brig *Statsraad Erichsen* (but she is not a brig, despite her small size—she is a full-rigged ship, with square sails on all three masts, another feature that sets her apart). The ship weighs 696 gross tons. Her length overall is 241 feet, with a hull length of 205 feet, a beam of 33 feet, five inches and a draft of 14 feet, nine inches. She carries 26 sails, having a total sail area of 13,280 square feet. As built, the ship had a 450-horsepower diesel engine that gave her a speed of only eight knots under power. Her complement included a captain, first, second and third officers, six instructors, a doctor, engineer, cook and steward, plus a crew of ten and 88 cadets.

The life of the *Christian Radich* has been anything but placid. Before World War II, the ship made two long voyages, the second of which brought her to the 1939 New York World's Fair. Despite the obvious approach of war, the *Christian Radich* sailed home and joined the Norwegian fleet at the Horten naval base. The Germans tried to win Norwegian cooperation to use the ship for training in the Baltic. Eventually they seized her and made her a submarine depot ship. At the war's end, she was found, half sunken, at Flensburg, just north of the German border in Denmark. Raised by the Allies and returned to her owners, she was rebuilt at Sandefjord and returned to service. Alf Bjercke, a business and civic leader in Oslo, became her patron. He arranged for her to be the star in the film *Windjammer,* seen by millions all over the world. The vessel was again given a major refit, including a more powerful engine. Still under the guidance of Alf Bjercke, she joined the two other active Norwegian training ships *Sørlandet* and *Statsraad Lehmkuhl* and sailed in 1964 to New York for the first OpSail, returning in 1976 and in 1986 for the second and third New York OpSails. En route home in 1976, a severe storm blew out her sails and forced her master to send out an S.O.S., but before help arrived, control was reestablished and she returned home under bare spars.

ABOVE: *The* Christian Radich *at the Bicentennial Operation Sail, 1976.* OVERLEAF: *The* Christian Radich's *training crew at work.*

ABOVE: *The* Christian Radich.

# *Corsaro II*

The handsome Italian naval sail-training yawl *Corsaro II,* designed by the famous American naval architectural firm of Sparkman & Stephens, was built in 1960 at Genoa and is an important member of the Italian Navy's sail program. Her home port is La Spezia. She measures 68 feet, nine inches overall. Her beam is 15 feet, four inches and she has a draft of 9.6 feet. Her main mast is 83 feet above sea level. She can do seven knots with her 110-horsepower diesel engine. Four officers, a crew of five and seven cadets make up her complement. She participated in the OpSails of 1964, 1976 and 1986.

ABOVE: *The* Corsaro II.

# *Cuauhtémoc*

Built in 1982, when oil money enriched Mexico, this fine vessel is one of four sister ships launched at the same shipyard—Astilleros y Talleres, of Bilbao, Spain. The proud flagship of the training fleet of the Mexican Navy, she is based at Vera Cruz on the East Coast and Acapulco on the West Coast. Like her sister ships, she is bark-rigged. Her length overall is 296 feet, ten inches, and she has a beam of 39 feet with a draft of 17 feet, eight inches. Her sail area is 27,757 square feet. Her complement includes 24 officers and a crew of 85, in addition to 90 cadets.

The *Cuauhtémoc* was named after the last Aztec emperor, who was defeated by the Spaniard Cortés and his conquistadors. In appearance she is clean-cut and modern looking. A gilded figurehead of the Aztec emperor rises from a modest gold-leaf decorative scroll running aft on either side of the stem. A modern black anchor fits into the hawsehole. The ship's name is in unusually large letters of a distinctive design just aft of some more gold leaf forward on the forecastle. Two good-sized lifeboats, stained mahogany, hang from davits on either side of the poop. The hull's length is accentuated by a thin gold line running from the figurehead scrollwork all the way aft and around under the full counter stern. The white-hulled three-master has a tonnage of 1800 gross. Her mainmast rises 164 feet, six inches above the deck. A small diesel engine permits her to operate at ten knots under power. With sails alone she can make considerably more than this. This superb vessel was present with her three sisters (the *Gloria* of Colombia, the *Guayas* of Ecuador and the *Simón Bolívar* of Venezuela), together for the first and, it is believed, only time in their careers, at the 1986 Operation Sail at New York. A "Four Sisters" trophy has been created by the noted American sculptor Anthony Fabbricante to honor these four ships. Plans are under way for a race from Norfolk to Montauk Point, at the eastern end of Long Island, in 1994.

BELOW: *The* Cuauhtémoc.

# *Danmark*

Designed by Aage Larsen, the *Danmark* was launched on November 19, 1932, at the yard of Nakskov Skibs, Lolland, Denmark, and completed in the following year, in the depths of the Depression. Built by the state, she is operated by the Danish government to create a supply of well-trained officers for the privately operated Danish merchant marine. As originally constructed, she had space for 120 boys, some as young as 15 years of age. In 1959 the number was reduced to 80. Wherever possible, old-style features have been retained aboard. The double steering wheel, for example, has no mechanical aids; muscles must provide all the power to steer. Similarly, stock anchors instead of the more modern patent anchors are used, and the capstan is turned manually. Crew members have berths, but the boys use hammocks. The *Danmark* measures 252 feet, seven inches in overall length, has a beam of 32 feet, nine inches and a depth of 17 feet. Her 26 sails present a sail area of 17,610 square feet, but she has a 486-horsepower diesel able to move her under power at nine knots. The ship's tonnage is 790 tons gross and her homeport is Copenhagen.

In 1939, while the ship was in New York, her master, Captain Knud L. Hansen, was told to keep her in United States waters instead of risking a voyage home as war began. For nearly three years he maintained his ship and crew at Jacksonville, Florida, with the help of Danish-Americans. Immediately after Pearl Harbor, Captain Hansen called President Roosevelt to offer his ship to the United States to help train officers for American merchant ships. The President accepted and the *Danmark* became a U.S. Coast Guard sail-training ship at the Coast Guard Academy, New London, Connecticut. Aboard her, 5000 cadets were indoctrinated in the importance of "pulling together." The ship was returned to Denmark on November 13, 1945, and restored to her original duty the following year. The *Danmark* was given a lead position in the 1964 OpSail, a spot still reserved for her at New York tall-ship gatherings in recognition of her service under the Stars and Stripes in World War II. Many have attributed her long and successful career to the figurehead of Neptune with forked trident and horn at her bow. The *Danmark*'s work during World War II prompted the U.S. Coast Guard to acquire the tall ship *Horst Wessel,* renamed the *Eagle,* a German war reparation.

---

ABOVE, LEFT: *The figurehead of the* Danmark. ABOVE, RIGHT: *The* Danmark *under sail.*

# Dar Młodzieży

This new Polish steel sail-training ship is one of the world's largest. Her name, "gift of youth" in Polish, was given because funds for her construction were raised by a public subscription from the young people of Poland. Built at Gdańsk (formerly Danzig) in 1982, she is 356 feet long and has a gross of 2946 tons. She is one of a class of big ships that has been built in Poland in recent years. A full-rigged ship, she has a sail area of 31,600 square feet. Her mainmast rises 163 feet above the deck. The ship has a complement of 135, including 90 trainees. A highly steeved bowsprit makes for a beautiful forward section, but a squared-off transom gives her stern a less than attractive appearance. On her long, uninterrupted main deck, large gravity davits for the *Dar Młodzieży's* big lifeboats give a feeling of clutter, but they are important for safety. The vessel is operated by the Polish Merchant Navy School. Rather than going into naval service, as is the case with men learning on many other training ships, the ship's officers trained on her decks will serve aboard the country's large fleet of merchant ships.

BELOW: *The* Dar Młodzieży. RIGHT: *Manning the spars aboard the* Dar Młodzieży.

# *Dewarutji*

The *Dewarutji* was built in 1952 by H. C. Stulcken & Son, of Hamburg. She was first operated by the Indonesian Naval Academy at Surabaya; later she made her home port at Djakarta. With square yards on her foremast only, the *Dewarutji* is classed as a barkentine. Her overall length is 191 feet, three inches, and her beam is 29.6 feet. She has a draft of 13 feet. Her 946-horsepower diesel "take home" engine (used only in emergencies) allows her a speed under power of 12.8 knots. The vessel has a gross tonnage of 931.7 tons. Her hull is usually painted gray, with a white strake below the spar deck. Her complement includes 15 officers and a crew of 67, plus 64 cadets. The *Dewarutji* has a sail area of 11,739 square feet. The name, from the Hindu epic poem *Mahabharata*, belongs to an Indonesian sea god depicted as the ship's colorful wooden figurehead. The entire vessel is air-conditioned, vital in her part of the world. To come to OpSail in 1964, she circumnavigated the world, departing in March and getting home the following December.

This interesting vessel shocked our small team of workers during her trip by cabling us that she had suffered an accident in the Suez Canal en route. Her main topmast was damaged, but somehow along the way the crew of brave Indonesians made the needed repairs and she arrived in fine shape for the July 14 parade up New York harbor.

ABOVE: *The* Dewarutji. OVERLEAF: *The* Dewarutji, *1964.*

ABOVE: *The* Dewarutji.

# *Druzhba*

The 365-foot *Druzhba* was built in 1987 in Poland as a sister to the *Dar Młodzieży*. In 1990, 30 U.S. merchant-marine trainee cadets went to Odessa to sail with about 100 young Soviet trainees on the first joint U.S.–U.S.S.R. merchant sail-training cruise. The two-month, 6500-mile trip was an eye-opener to them all. Two American organizations, Deepwater Alliance and Ocean Voyages, worked out details with the Odessa Maritime Academy helped by Ed Kane, a partner in an American trading firm in the Black Sea port. Captain Richard D. "Red" Shannon, a retired U.S. Coast Guard officer and frequent master of the famous four-masted tall ship *Sea Cloud,* signed on as training director with four officers from the National Oceanic and Atmospheric Administration, and the great adventure happened.

Off Bermuda a brush with Hurricane Bertha saw fierce winds and waves up to 12 feet high, but otherwise the ship cruised without incident via Turkey, Spain, the Canary Islands and Bermuda before reaching Baltimore, her first American port. Not only were many friendships made (the ship's name means "friendship") and a new understanding gained, but many precedents were set. Although no woman, for example, had ever been permitted to enlist in the Russian Navy, Cindy Smith, who teaches navigation at the Texas Maritime Academy in Galveston, was assigned aboard the *Druzhba* as course-plotting navigator. She brought three Soviet officials back to Texas with her to help set up the next joint cadet-training cruise.

ABOVE, TOP AND BOTTOM: *The* Druzhba.

# *Eagle*

The *Eagle,* America's most famous tall ship, was for many years the only active large sail-training ship in the United States. She has been host ship for all three OpSail events at New York. This beautiful and distinguished vessel, built in Germany by Blohm & Voss, Hamburg, was launched June 30, 1936 as the *Horst Wessel,* a name chosen by Adolf Hitler. The *Eagle* is 295 feet long, 39 feet in beam and has a draft of 17 feet. She has a sail area of 21,345 square feet with 22 sails. The fore and mainmasts are 150 feet above the waterline, while the fore and main yards are 78.6 feet long. A complement of 19 officers, 46 crew members and 180 cadets make up the ship's company on training cruises. She usually takes two

cruises each summer, giving the Coast Guard Academy's first and third classes a long voyage to Central America or Europe, and a shorter cruise for the second and fourth classes. Cadets sleep in hammocks.

Her hull coloring, with its slash of red, white, blue and gold painted across the bows, made her a topic of conversation. The color scheme originated some years earlier as a means of quick identification for small Coast Guard vessels. The idea had been conceived of by President Kennedy, who had been wondering how he could spot help if needed for his large family of children, nieces and nephews when they might be swimming off their compound

on Cape Cod. The Coast Guard commissioned an ad agency to come up with an emblem that could be quickly spotted from a distance. They devised the striking slash, cutting across the white hull of small Coast Guard vessels. In 1975 Admiral Owen Siler, Commandant in Washington, decided that it was so distinctive that it should also be put on the *Eagle*. His action created a loud protest from sail purists, but the slash has remained. Most people like it now. The *Eagle* is one of the famous "Five Sisters," the other four being the *Tovarisch* (launched May 3, 1933 as the *Gorch Fock*); the Portuguese *Sagres II* (launched October 30, 1937); the *Mircea* of Roumania (launched September 1938) and Germany's new *Gorch*

*Fock II* (launched December 17, 1958). The five were together for the first time, it is believed, in the 1976 Bicentennial OpSail. A special silver trophy cup was created for that occasion. It was won by the *Gorch Fock II*. In September 1986, on the ship's fiftieth birthday, a beautiful trophy sculpted by Anthony Fabbricante was presented to the *Eagle* at ceremonies at the South Street Seaport Museum, Pier 15, New York City.

OPPOSITE: *The* Eagle, *showing her distinctive stripe.* ABOVE: *The* Eagle *at New York, a Moran tug in the foreground.* OVERLEAF: *The* Eagle *under sail.*

ABOVE: *The* Eagle

# Esmeralda

The *Esmeralda* became the third-largest sail-training ship in the world by an accident. Laid down in 1946 at Cádiz, Spain, by the Echevarrieta y Larrinaga shipyard, she was intended as an exact sister ship of the *Juan Sebastián de Elcano* of 1927. Her name was to have been *Juan d'Austria,* but she was badly damaged by fire and abandoned. In 1952 she was launched to get her out of the way. She was acquired by Chile and completed in 1954 as a four-masted barkentine with a length, including bowsprit, of 370.10 feet—just ten inches longer than the *Juan Sebastián.* At that point she was surpassed in overall length, including bowsprit, by only the *Sedov* and *Kruzenshtern.* She was named *Esmeralda,* in honor of a Chilean warship which had won fame in Chile's Nitrate War with Bolivia and Peru. Her beam remained the same as that of the Spanish ship. The height of the mainmast is 159 feet above the waterline, compared to 150 feet for the *Juan Sebastián.* Her sail area was made 30,700 square feet, compared to 26,555 square feet for the Spanish four-master. The *Esmeralda* and her sister ship both carry the old schooner rig with all gaffs hoisted and lowered. The sails are attached to the four masts by hoops. The *Esmeralda* sets no fore-and-aft gaff sail on her foremast as does *Juan Sebastián,* so she is known as a barkentine, while the Spaniard is called a topsail schooner. The *Esmeralda* was given a longer forecastle, almost reaching the mainmast, during a reconstruction in 1954. The Chilean beauty has a crew of 21 officers and 222 men, while housing 95 cadets. Her homeport is Valparaíso.

During planning stages for both the 1976 and 1986 OpSail, our Board of Directors was pressured by many organizations, including Congress, to deny the *Esmeralda* a part in the New York parade. It was charged that the ship had been used as a "torture ship" by the repressive Chilean government. In 1975 and 1976 my office high up in One World Trade Center was invaded by hundreds of chanting people several times. We resisted these efforts, explaining that we were inviting the ships and their young cadets—not the governments of the countries participating. Our hope was that by seeing New York and meeting other seamen from all over the world, the young Chilean cadets would return home and influence their respective nations to become more democratic. On each occasion when the *Esmeralda* arrived at New York her decks were thronged by hundreds of thousands and her cadets were royally welcomed.

RIGHT: *The* Esmeralda. OVERLEAF: *The* Esmeralda *passes the Statue of Liberty, 1976.*

ABOVE: *The* Esmeralda.

# Georg Stage II

This is the second ship of the name built for the Georg Stage Memorial Foundation, created in 1882 by a Danish shipowner to honor his son, whose bust serves as the ship's figurehead. She was built by Frederikshavns Vaerft & Flydedok. Her hull is 134.6 feet long, her beam is 27.6 feet and her draft is 12.6 feet. Her 20 sails have an area of 9260 square feet. The 122-horsepower diesel engine below can drive the 298 gross-ton ship at a modest five knots. She has five watertight compartments and a double bottom, four lifeboats, one motorboat and a dinghy. Her starboard anchor is the old-fashioned kind with a stock, while she has a modern, stockless anchor to port. She has a crew of 13 for Atlantic voyages and can carry 80 trainees. Boys and girls are selected for training on this tiny full-rigged ship in February. Courses begin in April and a cruise visits ports in Sweden, Norway and Scotland during the summer. When she returns to her home port of Copenhagen in September, the young trainees unrig her. She is laid up at the Royal Danish Naval Yard during each winter. Some of the youngsters chosen for training are asked to pay a small sum for the experience, although some pay nothing or even receive a small subsidy. Graduates of one of her training courses often go on to the state-owned training ship *Danmark,* hoping to have a lifetime career at sea on Danish merchant ships. The program has had over a century of success, a tribute to good planning.

The ship visited the United States for the first time in 1989, calling at the American Merchant Marine Museum at the U.S. Merchant Marine Academy, Kings Point, New York.

RIGHT: Georg Stage II. BELOW: *The crew works on the deck of the Georg Stage II.*

# *Gladan*

*Gladan* (the kite) and *Falken* (the falcon), Sweden's twin gaff schooners, were built at Stockholm in 1946 and 1947, respectively, for the Royal Swedish Navy. Karlskrona is their home port. The vessels are of virtually identical schooner yacht design, with a spoon bow, very short bowsprit and rounded stern. Their gaff rig and the square yard on the foremast are their bow to traditional style. Each has a 220-ton displacement and an overall length of 128 feet, 11 inches, with an extreme beam of 23 feet, seven inches and a draft of 13 feet, nine inches. Both have one running square sail of 936 square feet in addition to their 5586 square feet of working sails. The masts have topmasts. The mainmasts rise 103 feet above the waterline. Each vessel can accommodate 38 trainees with a crew, including officers, of 15. The *Gladan* came to OpSail 1976; one or both of the two usually participate in the Sail Training Association's tall-ship races along the coast of Europe.

LEFT, TOP: *The* Falken, *the* Gladan's *sister ship.* LEFT, BOTTOM: *The* Gladan.

# Gloria

The *Gloria* was built in 1968 in Bilbao, Spain, at the shipyard of Astilleros y Talleres, the first of a series of four new barks. Her dimensions are: overall length, 249 feet, ten inches; beam, 39 feet, four inches; and draft 17 feet, eight inches. She has a gross tonnage of 1800 tons. Her mast rises 154.6 feet above the waterline. She can carry a crew of 85 with 24 officers and a cadet complement of 90. The steel-hulled vessel is painted the traditional white and she boasts three masts. The *Gloria,* which belongs to the Colombian Navy, has a sail area of 15,069 square feet. Her home port is Cartagena.

A great winged figurehead suggesting an angel is the ship's most distinctive decorative feature. Her silhouette is marred slightly by a large bridge mounted on a windowed cabin at the forward end of her poop. It is topped by a large square pilothouse with three huge windows facing forward, which detracts from the traditional design of an historic tall ship. It is doubtless very practical and makes the job of steering her much more comfortable than on ships with a more conventional outline. A good-sized diesel engine permits the *Gloria* to make ten knots under power. Because of her success as a national standard-bearer in OpSail 1976, three other tall ships were ordered. They are almost sister ships, although each was a little longer than the *Gloria.* The *Gloria*'s three sisters are Ecuador's *Guayas,* built in 1977 and 262 feet long; Venezuela's *Simón Bolívar,* built in 1979 and 270 feet long; and Mexico's *Cuauhtémoc,* built in 1982 and 296 feet in length.

RIGHT, TOP: *The* Gloria *in ceremonial display.* RIGHT, BOTTOM: *The* Gloria *at sea.*

# Gorch Fock II

This ship was the fifth of a kind, all built by the famous Hamburg shipyard of Blohm & Voss, where the great liner *Vaterland* (the ship that became America's most famous passenger ship, the *Leviathan*) was built in 1912–14. The first four were divided among the Allies at the end of World War II. They were named, in order of their construction: *Gorch Fock* (1933), *Horst Wessel* (1936), *Albert Leo Schlageter* (1937) and *Mircea* (1938). The *Gorch Fock II* was launched in 1958. The masthead of this superb tall ship rises 170 feet above sea level. Her figurehead is a golden eagle. She can carry 170 cadets and has 12 officers and a crew of 63. Her sail area is 21,011 square feet. Like her sisters, she is bark-rigged. Her length is 293 feet and her beam 39 feet. She has a gross of 1870 tons. Kiel is her home port. In 1974 I was able to raise enough money to buy a large silver trophy cup and arrange a special race of the five ships between Bermuda and Newport, Rhode Island. It was won by the *Gorch Fock II*.

BELOW: *The crew of the* Gorch Fock II *during foul weather.* OPPOSITE, TOP AND BOTTOM: *The* Gorch Fock II.

# *Guayas*

The second of the new "Four Sisters" is the *Guayas,* built in 1977 in Bilbao. She was christened in honor of the River Guayas, on which the Ecuadorian Naval Superior School is located at Guayaquil. This institution was founded in 1822 by Simón Bolívar. Her overall length is 262 feet, six inches, and her beam is 34 feet, eight inches. Her tonnage is variously listed as from 914 to 1153 tons. (Tonnage is measured in many different ways, and there are half a dozen different kinds of tonnage from gross to net. Each of the world's major waterways has different tonnage measurement rules, adding further confusion.) The *Guayas* has a 750-horsepower engine capable of driving her at nine knots under power. She can carry 60 to 80 naval cadets and has 15 officers with a crew of 73. Her sail area is 17,222 square feet, slightly greater than that of *Gloria.*

The *Guayas* is notable for her figurehead, a giant condor depicted in full flight. Her silhouette is almost identical to that of *Gloria,* except for the presence of a black line around the hull and a mahogany-stained bridge. The stain helps to make the bridge a little less obvious and improves the ship's overall appearance. The *Guayas* circumnavigated South America on her maiden voyage in 1978.

ABOVE AND OPPOSITE: *The* Guayas.

# *Iskra* and *Iskra II*

The *Iskra* of 1917 survived both world wars and served under three flags. Recently retired as a Polish sail-training ship, she was built by G. Muller, of Foxhol, Holland. Owned by a Dutch company, Zeevarts Maatschappij, she was first registered in Groningen and used for coastal cargo service under the name of *Vlissingen*. The Glasgow sailing-ship firm of A. Kennedy & Son bought her in 1925 and renamed her *St. Blane.* Two years later, Poland acquired the 170-foot vessel and transformed her to carry cadets as a Polish naval sail-training ship. Two deckhouses were built forward and aft and portholes were cut through the hull, giving her a completely different appearance. A square yard was rigged to her foremast, and she was renamed *Iskra* (flash).

When World War II began the ship was in French North Africa. She was acquired by the French. When France surrendered, the vessel was seized by the British Navy and became the H.M.S. *Iskra,* her home port being Gibraltar. Having served throughout the rest of the war as a supply ship, she was returned to Poland when peace came. Rebuilt again for sail training, the ship had four more decades of use. In her most recent period her sail area was 7320 square feet and she had 11 sails. Her mainmast rose 82 feet above the deck. Her beam was 25 feet, seven inches and she had a depth of 11 feet, ten inches. Her crew and cadet complement numbered 55 to 60. The ship's three masts were all the same height; each had a topmast. The vessel had a 260-horsepower diesel. Her displacement was 500 tons. In 1982 the new *Iskra II* was built as an identical sister ship of the *Pogoria* (*q.v.*). Sad to say, the 1917 *Iskra* has just faded away.

LEFT: *The* Iskra. BELOW: *The* Iskra II.

# Juan Sebastián de Elcano

The *Juan Sebastián de Elcano* probably does more sailing than any other major tall ship. As of 1986 she had circled the world six times. This is most appropriate, for she is named in honor of the first sailor to take a ship around the globe—Ferdinand Magellan's second in command on his historic trip circumnavigating the globe. (Magellan was killed in 1521, before he could complete the voyage.)

The *Juan Sebastián* was built by Echevarrieta y Larrinaga, of Cádiz. Her homeport is San Fernando, a part of Cádiz, and she is known as a four-masted topsail schooner, although she has yards and square sails on her foremast. She is one of the world's largest sailing vessels, boasting 20 sails with 26,555 square feet of canvas. Huge for sail, the ship is of 3750 tons displacement and has an overall length of 350 feet, six inches, not including a good part of her bowsprit. Her beam is 43 feet and her draft is 22 feet, seven

inches. Her masts are all of equal height, being 150 feet above her deck, or 160 feet over the waterline. As an example of the ship's remarkable size, her bowsprit is 63 feet in length. In addition to 89 cadets the vessel carries 243 officers, petty officers and crew. The officers live in paneled luxury and the huge wardroom far aft is rich and elegant. She is the property of the Spanish Navy. Her 1500-horsepower diesel can move her at nine knots. The ship boasts a beautiful figurehead of a woman wearing a crown. The *Juan Sebastián de Elcano* participated in all three Operation Sail parades into New York harbor.

---

ABOVE: *The* Juan Sebastián de Elcano *at the Bicentennial Operation Sail, 1976.* OVERLEAF: *The* Juan Sebastián de Elcano *in New York harbor.*

ABOVE: *The* Juan Sebastián de Elcano.

# Kruzenshtern

The *Kruzenshtern* was built as *Padua* in 1926 by J. C. Tecklenborg, at Wesermünde, for F. Laeisz. Her gross is 3545 tons. Her overall is 375.5 feet. She has a beam of 46 feet and a depth of 25. The ship was seized at Swinemünde in 1946 by the Soviets and renamed after the Russian explorer Adam Johann Ritter von Kruzenshtern (1770–1846).

In *Great Sailing Ships*, Otmar Schauffelen writes that the *Kruzenshtern* was the last cargo-carrying four-masted bark to be built, having been completed in 1926 for the noted Hamburg shipowner L. Laeisz. Contrary to most thinking of that time, Laeisz saw that there was a place for very large sailing ships in the transportation of bulk cargoes on long overseas routes. He had bought and refitted a number of such ships after World War I. The *Kruzenshtern* was his thinking as expressed in a brand-new ship.

He used her to carry nitrates and grain. She was a traditional Laeisz three-island ship, with forecastle, Liverpool deck and poop. As built she had no engine. From the outset she was used as both a cargo ship and a training ship for boys learning to become ship officers. This dual function was part of the Laeisz philosophy. The 40 berths for trainees were always filled. Long voyages marked the ship's career as a cargo carrier. Her first passage, from Hamburg to Talcahuano, Chile, took 87 days outbound and 94 days return. Even without engines, in 1933–34 she made a record trip of 67 days from Hamburg to Port Lincoln, South Australia. She participated in the 1976 Operation Sail and again in the 1986 event honoring the centenary of the Statue of Liberty.

---

ABOVE AND OVERLEAF, TOP AND BOTTOM: *The* Kruzenshtern.

ABOVE: *The* Kruzenshtern.

# La Belle Poule
and *L'Étoile*

France has two small wooden schooners serving as their sail-training ships. *La Belle Poule* ("the beautiful hen") and *L'Étoile* ("the star") were built in 1932 by Chantiers Navals de Normandie, Fécamp. Owned by the French navy, their home port is Brest. Both masts on each have topmasts. Their tonnage is 227 displacement. Each is 123 feet overall, with a beam of 23 feet, seven inches and a draft of 11 feet, ten inches. They each have nine sails with a sail area of 4560 square feet. Their complement consists of three officers, five petty officers, 12 crew and 30 cadets. *La Belle Poule* is the fourth French naval vessel to bear this name. The first was a pirate ship that gave valuable help to the French Navy. The continued use of the name for French craft was ordered by Louis XV. Another predecessor of that name brought the exhumed body of Napoleon back to France in 1840, 19 years after his death. *L'Étoile* is the fifteenth ship to bear the name since 1622. Both ships saved themselves from the Germans during World War II by taking refuge in Portsmouth.

RIGHT, TOP: *The* Belle Poule. RIGHT, BOTTOM: L'Étoile.

# Libertad

The *Libertad* was commissioned on May 28, 1960, seven years after the keel had been laid. The work was done at Río Santiago, Argentina, by the A.F.N.E. Astilleros Navales, the Argentine state shipyard, and the 3092-ton ship was a monument to its skills. The *Libertad*'s six-month maiden voyage in the summer of 1963 took her from Buenos Aires to San Juan, Bermuda, Lisbon, Le Havre, Hamburg, London, Cádiz and Dakar. During her visit at Hamburg, 30,000 visitors toured her; twice that number saw her at New York in 1964.

In 1966 the *Libertad* distinguished herself by winning the transatlantic speed record for sail on a passage from Canada to the British Isles. The *Libertad* is a huge vessel. All three of her topmasts reach 159 feet, six inches into the sky. She has a sail area of 28,450 square feet, with 27 sails. Her overall length is 365 feet, making her longer than nearly all the older tall ships. Her beam is 44 feet, four inches and her draft 21 feet, ten inches. With twin 1200-horsepower diesels, she can make 13.5 knots under power. The *Libertad* has 25 officers, a crew of 167 and usually carries 171 cadets. She has a full hull and rounded cruiser-type stern decorated with the arms of the Argentine Navy. A gilded figurehead was added to the stem soon after the ship entered service. A large bridge and pilothouse are forward and a single small smokestack rises aft. The large lifeboats and other deck clutter hide these modern structures and they are hardly noticed. The *Libertad* is a full-rigged ship.

LEFT AND BELOW: *The* Libertad.

# *Mircea*

One of the five sisters built by Blohm & Voss in Hamburg, Germany, this lovely steel bark was ordered by the Romanian Navy in 1938. She has an unusual figurehead (a man, instead of the more traditional woman) depicting the Walachian Prince Mircea the Old, who rewon the Dobruja region from Turkey in the fourteenth century. He is carved with his mustache, gilded crown and shield. The ship's appearance is also distinguished by her large smokestack rising between the main and mizzenmasts—something that traditional sailors frown on. Her overall length is 269.5 feet, her beam is 39 feet, 5 inches and she has a sail area of 18,815 square feet. Although her complement changes frequently, she usually carries about 40 officers, 120 apprentices and a crew of 50. The *Mircea*'s home port is Constanţa, on the Black Sea. She is a true tall ship,

with a mainmast that towers 161 feet, 4 inches above the bottom of her keel, 133 feet, 3 inches from her deck. Her rig includes 23 sails—4 headsails (jibs), double topsails, single topgallants, royals, a double spanker and gaff topsail on her mizzenmast. The four other sisters of this historic quintette are the U.S. Coast Guard's *Eagle,* the *Sagres II,* of Portugal, the German *Gorch Fock* (now the Russian *Tovarisch*) and the current German sail-training ship built in 1958 and named *Gorch Fock II.* A sixth ship of this type was never named. Loaded with wartime gas shells after World War II, she was sunk in the Baltic.

ABOVE: *The* Mircea.

# Nippon Maru and
# Kaiwo Maru

Each of these ships was a spectacular four-master, each a beauty, each had been built in 1930. They were 318 feet long, had a 42-foot, six-inch beam and a draft of 22 feet. Built in Kobe by the Kawasaki Yard, when in service each could carry 27 officers, a crew of 48 plus 120 cadets. Their mainmasts rose 145 feet over the deck, and each had 25,800 square feet of sail with 22 sails. Both were rigged as four-masted steel barks and each had a gross of 2285 tons. In design they differed from many other tall ships because their poop decks were extended forward almost to the forecastle. This made the "awning deck" 213 feet long. It could accommodate six large lifeboats. The navigation bridge was between the fore and mainmasts. The upper bridge had a steering wheel; there was another in the wheelhouse below. The traditional double wheel for manual steering was aft of the jigger or fourth mast. Everything was done in the traditional way. But a large squat smokestack could be seen between the main and mizzenmasts. This, plus the two rows of portholes in the big hull, made the ships look like old-style clipper-bowed passenger ships of the late nineteenth century. The *Nippon Maru* is now laid up as a tourist attraction.

ABOVE: *The* Kaiwo Maru. OPPOSITE: *The* Nippon Maru *in San Francisco Bay.*

# *Nippon Maru II* and *Kaiwo Maru II*

The era of great tall ships is not dead—far from it, as evidenced by activity in Japan. Two new four-masted square-rigged barks are flying the Japanese flag. The *Nippon Maru II,* the first, was finished in 1984. A sister, *Kaiwo Maru II,* came out in 1989. Both were built by the Sumitomo Heavy Industries, Ltd., shipyard at Yososuka, Japan. The *Nippon Maru II* is of 2570 gross tons while the *Kaiwo Maru II* is a bit smaller. Each has a length of 361.2 feet and a beam of 45.3 feet. Each has 36 sails offering a tremendous 29,708 feet of sail area. They carry 70 officers and 120 cadets and have twin 1500-horse-power diesel engines.

A gilded figurehead with some scrollwork gives the ship's bow the proper traditional feel. The poop, Liverpool deck amidships and forecastle are all united into one continuous upper deck. The mast height of 155 feet gives the two sister ships superb proportions. Their jigger-mast canvas is divided into three sails easily handled. The only features that mark the *Nippon Maru II* and the *Kaiwo Maru II* as modern vessels are the anchors pulled up tight to the twin hawseholes on their bows. The older sisters had the traditional stock anchors suspended from the forecastle deck. The *Nippon Maru II* participated in the 1988 Australian Bicentennial.

LEFT, TOP: *The* Nippon Maru II. LEFT, BOTTOM: *The* Kaiwo Maru II.

# *Pogoria*

It is quite remarkable how the Polish have turned out tall ships in recent years. Both the *Pogoria* and the *Iskra II* are 154 feet long, with a 26-foot beam and a draft of 11 feet. Their three masts rise 114 feet above the waterline. Each was built in Gdańsk, and has eight officers, a crew of 41 and 50 cadets. Each ship's sail area comes to 10,736 square feet. Each has a 310-horsepower diesel. They are owned by the Interstar Yachting S.A., of Warsaw. The *Pogoria* and the *Iskra II* illustrate the resurgence of the tall ship and the bravery of Poland. Built in 1980, the *Pogoria* marked one of the first steps taken in Poland to defy the country's Communist government. Polish seamen dramatized their opposition to Red domination by creating the Iron Shackle Fraternity, a society whose iron-shackle symbol referred to the repressive regime. It was displayed for the world to see on the five square sails of the foremast of the *Pogoria* and the *Iskra II*. This and the pronounced cruiser stern set the design of these ships apart from that of all other tall ships—exactly what her naval architects wanted.

With a barkentine rig (square sails on the foremast only) and a blue stripe around their otherwise white hulls, the *Pogoria* and *Iskra II* stood out as an appeal to the world against Soviet oppression. The *Pogoria* was seen worldwide: She sailed to Antarctica, circumnavigated Africa and came to New York for the 1986 OpSail as a representative of Canada. Because official permission was delayed, the ship missed the parade entirely.

ABOVE: *The* Pogoria.

# Sagres II

For the past three decades this ship, as the *Sagres II,* of Portugal, has been the easiest tall ship to identify because, in accordance with Portuguese tradition, highly distinctive red crosses appear on the sails. She was launched October 30, 1937, at the famed Blohm & Voss shipyard, Hamburg, as the German Navy's sail-training ship *Albert Leo Schlageter.* Damaged by mines during World War II, the vessel was seized at Bremerhaven by the United States when the war ended. Since America already had her sister ship, the current *Eagle,* in 1948 the *Albert Leo Schlageter* was turned over to Brazil, becoming their *Guanabara,* used as a naval training ship until 1961. Sold to the Portuguese, she was renamed after the port in southern Portugal from which Henry the Navigator sent out his vessels of discovery to find a way around Africa. Her figurehead, originally an eagle, has been replaced by a bust of Henry. Owned by the Portuguese Navy, she has her home port at Alfeite, near Lisbon.

The ship makes two training cruises each year. She carries 90 cadets, 131 as crew and 29 officers. Her mainmast rises 146 feet above the waterline. Her dimensions: length 293 feet, beam 39 feet and draft 24 feet. Her 23 sails have an area of 19,132 square feet. A three-masted steel bark of 1784 gross tons, she has a 750-horsepower diesel and can make ten knots without her sails. Her white hull is decorated with a blue stripe. The sails on her mizzen are divided into three small fore-and-aft shaped sails. A small smoke-exhaust pipe is fitted at the forward end of the long poop, which extends almost up to the mainmast. Four large lifeboats, two to a side, hang from davits or rest atop a small deckhouse at the after end of the forecastle.

ABOVE: *The* Sagres II.

# *Sedov*

The bark *Sedov* was for years a perfect illustration of the breakdown of the Soviet system, laid up for over a decade in a Russian shipyard, undergoing a "restoration" that, in fact, was not being carried out. The world is fortunate that this great four-master was saved at all. Built in 1921 by Germania Werft (Krupp), at Kiel, she was a combination cargo-carrying and sail-training ship owned originally by F. A. Vinnen as *Magdalene Vinnen.* She was first used to import nitrates from South America.

In 1936 the North German Lloyd, long one of Germany's two best-known Atlantic liner companies, bought her for the Australian grain trade and officer training. She ran under the name of *Kommander Johnsen.* In 1939, her last long voyage under the German flag, from Australia to Cobh, took 107 days. During World War II she ran for a time in the Baltic, eventually being laid up in Flensburger Fjord. After hostilities, she flew the British flag for a while and was then turned over to the Soviets, who renamed her *Sedov* in honor of the Russian polar explorer Georgij J. Sedov (1877–1914). Under Soviet control she had a white hull, quite unlike the black hull with its white band and imitation gun ports of the equally famous *Kruzenshtern.* With the coming of *glasnost,* the ship was used to earn hard currency by selling passage to young

people willing to work alongside Soviet trainees. With the dissolution of the Soviet Union, she now belongs to Latvia.

The *Sedov*'s overall length, from the tip of her bowsprit to her aftermost extremity, is 385 feet, seven inches. She has a gross of 3476 tons and a beam of 48 feet. Her mainmast rises 178 feet, ten inches over her deck, making her the tallest of the tall ships. Her four masts can accommodate 34 sails, accounting for her tremendous 45,121 square feet of canvas. Her complement includes a crew of 70 and 164 cadets. All her masts have topmasts and she carries royals on her three forward masts, but not skysails. Like the *Kruzenshtern,* she is a three-island ship, meaning that her superstructure features three structures above the hull—the poop far aft, the Liverpool deck amidships and a forecastle. Her main steering wheel is forward of the charthouse on the Liverpool deck. An emergency wheel is placed in the traditional position far aft, where custom has dictated, from the days of the most ancient Greek ships, that all proper steering should take place. This wheel is raised slightly and has a skylight above it to permit the helmsman to see the pull of the wind on the sails.

ABOVE: *The* Sedov.

# Simón Bolívar

The third of the new "Four Sisters," the *Simón Bolívar* represented a decided departure in appearance from the first two. On the new Venezuelan ship, the large bridge structure aft was eliminated, giving the ship's outline a more traditional and a more pleasing look. Another striking difference is the dark stripe painted around the ship's hull at the main-deck level, leaving the raised forecastle, poop and lower hull white. Below this strake is a line of imitation gun ports, similar to those painted on the French *Belem*.

As were the other three of the four sisters, the *Simón Bolívar* was built in Bilbao, Spain. Her overall length is 270 feet. Her beam is just under 35 feet and she has a draft of 17 feet. The ship's gross is 1248 tons. A 700-horsepower diesel can move her at ten knots. The ship has a complement of 17 officers and 51 seamen and can carry 42 cadets. Her figurehead is of a figure of Liberty.

ABOVE, TOP AND BOTTOM: *The* Simón Bolívar.

# Sir Winston Churchill and *Malcolm Miller*

The keel of the graceful three-masted schooner *Sir Winston Churchill* was laid on November 21, 1964. Just before her launch, late in 1965, high winds toppled her over on the ways, breaking her masts. She was quickly righted, however, and entered service four months later, as scheduled.

On March 23, 1967, a donation from Sir James Miller, a former Lord Mayor of London and the Lord Provost of Edinburgh, enabled the Sail Training Association to lay the keel for a second vessel, *Malcolm Miller,* named after the donor's son, who had died in 1966 in an auto crash. The two vessels carry both women and men. The *Sir Winston Churchill*'s figurehead is of a red lion holding the S.T.A.'s shield. The *Malcolm Miller* has the coat of arms of the donor. Each is 150 feet overall, has a beam of 25 and a draft of 15 feet, six inches. The three masts, all of equal height, rise 97 feet, nine inches above the deck and are made of aluminum—each of one piece. There are 7104 square feet of working sail area in the 14 sails each ship carries. Portsmouth is home port for these sleek beauties. Each has a crew of seven and 40 boys and girls. The *Sir Winston Churchill* was built by Richard Dunston, Ltd., Haven Shipyard, Hessie, Hull, England. The *Malcolm Miller* came from the yards of John Lewis & Sons, Ltd., Aberdeen, Scotland. In a typical year the two British schooners carry 1260 young people on 30 cruises.

BELOW: *The* Sir Winston Churchill. RIGHT: *The* Malcolm Miller.

# Sørlandet

Two of the three current Norwegian sail-training vessels are full-rigged ships, quite unusual in today's world of sailing. A full-rigged ship fits square sails on all her masts. Both the *Christian Radich,* of Oslo, and the *Sørlandet,* of Kristiansand, have this once-standard feature, which entails more work for the cadets aboard. It entitles the craft to be officially listed as a "ship"—not just a bark or another classification. The *Sørlandet* ("southern land") started life in 1927 as one ship among many. Today only eight of the world's sail-training vessels are full-rigged ships. She was built by P. Höivolds mek. Verksted A/S, of Kristiansand and was until recently owned by her original owners, the Sørlandets Seilende Skoleskips Institution. The ship is now owned by the city of Kristiansand.

For many years the *Sørlandet* was the only major sail-training ship without an engine—a condition imposed by A. O. T. Skelbred, who funded the vessel. However, in 1959, a 240-horsepower diesel was installed—an affront to purists. The *Sørlandet* has 26 sails with a sail area of 10,765 square feet. Although her training cruises are usually in the Baltic and North Seas, in 1933 she visited the Chicago World's Fair, making a number of stops along the way via the St. Lawrence River and the Great Lakes. In 1964 she was one of the 11 major tall ships that visited New York for OpSail. Her cadets pay nothing for the training, the purpose of the ship being to provide more officers for the Norwegian merchant service.

BELOW: *The* Sørlandet.

# *Statsraad Lehmkuhl*

Unlike many ships of her type, the *Statsraad Lehmkuhl* has served as a sail-training ship for almost her entire life, having been launched in 1914. She was laid down by J. C. Tacklenborg, of Bremerhaven, as a three-masted bark. Originally named *Grossherzog Friedrich August,* she was built for the Deutscher Schulschiff-Verein as its third large training ship to provide officers for the vast pre–World War I German merchant marine.

The 1701-gross-ton vessel has 21 sails with a sail area of 21,528 square feet. The ship's overall length is 321 feet, her beam is 41 and her draft is 16 feet. One of the tallest of all today's tall ships, her mainmast towers 164 feet over the waterline. A crew of 24 and 180 cadets have usually sailed her. The *Statsraad Lehmkuhl* made Bergen her home port in 1922. During World War II she was seized by the Germans, renamed *Westwärts* (westward) and used as a naval depot ship. Returned to Norway in 1945, she continued as a sail-training ship until she was laid up in 1967. In 1988 she was restored and continues out of Bergen in limited use. With the decline of traditional merchant marines, maintaining her has become most difficult. To help pay her bills, she carries young passengers who are willing to assist with the chores of the ship.

ABOVE: *The* Statsraad Lehmkuhl.

# *Tovarisch*

On May 3, 1933, this graceful hull, named *Gorch Fock,* slipped into the waters from one of Blohm & Voss's ways at Hamburg, one of six nearly identical sister ships. In the war she was sunk in May 1945, off Stralsund, and remained on the bottom until 1948, when she was salvaged by the Russians. After 1951 she served the Soviet Union's navy and merchant marine as the *Tovarisch,* with her home port at Odessa. She is now owned by Cherson Merchant Marine School, Ukraine. Originally she carried 180 cadets and 66 officers and crew. She is 269 feet in length, 39 in beam and 17 in draft. Her gross is 1392 tons. The ship has 23 sails boasting an 18,400-square-foot sail area. Her mainmast rises 98 feet above the deck.

BELOW: *The* Tovarisch.

# *Zawisza Czarny*

Built in 1952 by Stocznia Północna, at Gdańsk, Poland, the 164-ton three-masted schooner has a length of 144 feet, a beam of 22 feet and a draft of 15 feet. She hoists ten sails with a combined area of 6835 square feet, according to a recent Japanese work about the world's major tall ships of today. Her name was derived from that of an ancient Polish noble family. The word "czarny" means "black one," and described a Pole who won fame defending his nation against the Teutonic Knights. His bust is the figurehead. The British had a nickname for this ship—"whiskey Johnny."

ABOVE: *The* Zawisza Czarny.

# Private Vessels

# Barba Negra

A Baltic trading schooner, the ship was built in 1896 in Hemne, Norway, and flew the Norwegian flag under another name as a whaler and a fishing vessel. In 1970 the craft was acquired by Albert Seidl and given the name *Barba Negra* (black beard). He rerigged her as a barkentine for the West Indies trades. He gave her a white stripe and imitation gun ports to make her fit the public's idea of an old-time sailing ship. Her own natural sheer and three masts made her ideal for various moving-picture assignments and she was in various European gatherings of tall ships, making some money from occasional special parties and assignments. The ship has managed to survive at Savannah, Georgia.

As rebuilt, the ship's overall length is 110 feet. She has a beam of 23 feet and a draft of 12 feet. With a tonnage of 55 gross, the *Barba Negra* requires a complement of three officers and five crew and can carry five cadets. Of wooden construction, she is a most colorful, romantic-looking ship. Her owner's cabin, far aft, occupies the entire poop, but is still barely large enough to fit a large double bed on gimbals. The amidships is entirely open and serves as a comparatively large general room, with a good-sized table, also on gimbals, in the center, surrounded by long benches, which become berths at night.

LEFT, TOP AND BOTTOM: *The* Barba Negra.

# *Bel Espoir II*

Originally the *Nette S.,* later the *Peder Most,* this vessel was built in 1944 for A. C. Sørensen to carry cattle between Denmark and Germany, having space for 200 head per trip. The wooden ship had three masts, each with topmasts, and nine sails spreading 5005 square feet. The mainmast's height was 80 feet. Gaff-rigged, her sails were bent to the masts with old-style hoops. In 1955 the vessel was bought by the famed Outward Bound Trust of London, which renamed it *Prince Louis II,* intending that the ship create character and stimulate a happy life-style for the 24 boys she carried. She proved too small for the assignment and was again sold in 1968. Her new owners were Les Amis de Jeudi–Dimanche, a French drug-treatment effort whose name is derived from the French school plan, which gives students half of each Thursday off for some special project. Home port for the ship was Le Havre. The ship is 120 feet in overall length, 23 feet in beam, 8.6 feet in draft. Her gross was listed as 189 tons.

ABOVE: *The* Bel Espoir II.

# *Bill of Rights*

Without any doubt one of the most beautiful sailing ships in the world today, the *Bill of Rights* was designed by McCurdy & Rhodes, who modeled her after the traditional American coastal schooner of the late nineteenth century. Harvey F. Gamage, whose name has been given to another sleek modern schooner replica, built the *Bill of Rights* at South Bristol, Maine. She was designed for commercial work carrying both sail-training crews and passengers out of Newport, Rhode Island. Another vessel similar to this beauty is the *Shenandoah,* also built by Gamage. The *Bill of Rights* is 151 feet long overall, has a beam of 24.6 feet and a draft of ten. Her sail area is 6300 square feet and her mainmast stands 115 feet above the

deck. The wooden-hulled beauty has a tonnage of 160 gross. She requires four officers and a crew of eight and has room for 30 cadets. She has no power. The wonderful rake to her two masts and her lovely hull lines give the *Bill of Rights* much of her breathtaking style and beauty. Her bowsprit is not raised, but continues with the same soft rise of the forward part of her graceful hull. Two traditional anchors are forward, adding to the feeling of simplicity of design. Low deck structures accentuate the sleekness.

ABOVE: *The* Bill of Rights.

# Black Pearl

This little brigantine was built as the private yacht of shipbuilder C. Lincoln Vaughn, of Wickford, Rhode Island. It is said that she averaged 8.1 knots during a 1160-mile summer cruise in 1965, and that she can be sailed by only two people. A slightly heavy-looking craft, she was bought in 1959 by Barclay H. Warburton, of Newport, who for a time headed the American Sail Training Association. He fitted her out to serve as a sail-training ship for four boys. The little vessel has ten sails with a total area of 1991 square feet. Her mainmast rises 55 feet above the deck. Her gross is calculated at 27 tons. Her overall length comes to 72.6 feet. She has a beam of 15.6 feet and a draft of eight feet. The *Black Pearl* has done much in her 40-year career, and has always been regarded as an outstanding sailer. Currently, she makes short trips up and down the East Coast with trainees aboard.

ABOVE: *The* Black Pearl.

# *Bluenose II*

The most famous of all Canadian schooners was the *Bluenose*, which took her name from the blue skin of a locally produced potato. (In the past, Nova Scotians were known as "bluenosers.") The original *Bluenose*, operating as a fishing boat between 1921 and 1938, was called the "Queen of the North Atlantic." Every summer she would compete with the finest American Gloucester-men, frequently winning the Fishermen's Cub Race. She sailed out of Halifax, and will be best remembered as having been used in the film *Captains Courageous,* starring Lionel Barrymore and Spencer Tracy. Her namesake, the *Bluenose II,* was built from the same plans and by the same builder as the original vessel. She slid down the ways at the Smith & Rhuland, Ltd., shipyard, Lunenburg, Nova Scotia, on February 27, 1963.

With an overall length of 161 feet, a beam of 27 and a draft of 16 feet, the *Bluenose II* is by no means a small vessel. Her eight sails combine to give 10,901 square feet of canvas. The height of her mainmast (above the deck) is 127 feet. A gaff-rigged vessel, she has only a small stump of a bowsprit extending forward from her rounded stem. She usually has a crew of 12 and can accommodate 12 cadets or passenger-guests. She is now owned by the Nova Scotia Department of Tourism. For the past three decades she has been Nova Scotia's ambassador of good will and Canada's most distinguished tall ship. She visited New York for both the 1976 and 1986 OpSail parades.

BELOW AND OPPOSITE: *The* Bluenose II.

# *Bounty*

The renown of the *Bounty,* on which the famous mutiny took place in 1789, has produced a number of historic replicas of this ship. This replica was built at Lunenburg, Nova Scotia, in 1960. The ship is 169 feet overall, 30 feet longer than the original, a change made necessary because of the demands of the 1962 film version of *Mutiny on the Bounty,* for which she was built. Otherwise the vessel followed the original plans, preserved in London. Even the carved figurehead, a lady in riding costume, was described in the eighteenth-century specifications. The 120-ton replica had 18 sails, with 10,225 square feet of sail area. Her mainmast rose 103 feet, eight inches above the deck. The original ship had a crew of 45, while the replica needed only 26, as she had twin screws and a 2220-horsepower diesel.

Following her movie carrer, the *Bounty* was tied up at Flushing during the 1964 New York World's Fair. Then she sailed to St. Petersburg, Florida, and was for many years a successful tourist attraction.

---

ABOVE: *The* Bounty.

# Californian

In the United States there are now half a dozen plans to build working tall ships. One such proposal was successfully executed in 1984 when the 145-foot wooden replica *Californian* was completed. The brainchild of the Nautical Heritage Society of Dana Point, California, she is designed to serve the youth of California. The new vessel is a replica of the 1848 revenue cutter *C. W. Lawrence,* which was used up and down the California coast during the Gold Rush. Volunteers contribute an average of 14,000 hours yearly in support of the ship's eight professionals and the Heritage Society's lean staff of four paid hands. It is a working scheme, which other, more ambitious tall-ship projects might do well to copy. Steve Christman, the mastermind of the *Californian* effort, raised the $2.5 million needed to build her and keep public interest alive through each phase of the ship's construction. For example, when the question of a figurehead came up, he decided to find for a model a woman who had both Mexican and American heritage. The choice was television actress Catherine Bach. The figurehead had long, flowing hair and a crown and necklace of California poppies. It was unveiled in 1985 on the occasion of the ship's first sail with local sea cadets aboard. The name of the *Californian*'s home port, Sacramento, is on the stern in large letters along with two carvings of the state's golden bear and a magnificent eagle with widespread wings and a three-starred, red, white and blue shield.

A flyer of 1987 prices four "hands-on sailing programs" being offered. Groups of 16 young people could be taken on an 11-day cruise for $700 each. Twelve adults could enjoy four-day, three-night voyages for $595 each. As many as 45 people could be carried on four-hour cruises, including lunch and a year's membership in the Heritage Society, for $75 each. Finally, a four- or six-day cruise for one or two couples cost from $600 to $725 per person. The two staterooms used opened into the elegant "Governor's Cabin." Adults sailing on the *Californian* always receive a membership in the Society's "Ancient Mariner" Alumni Association. This imaginative merchandising package is one of the most successful used by any modern private tall ship.

BELOW AND OVERLEAF: *The* Californian.

ABOVE: *The* Californian.

102    *PRIVATE VESSELS*

# *Clearwater*

Another highly successful modern privately owned American tall ship is the *Clearwater*, the dream of folksinger and social activist Pete Seeger. The vessel, built in 1969 at the Harvey Gamage shipyard at South Bristol, Maine, recreates the Hudson River sloop, a individualistic ship type that evolved on the Hudson River. The roots of this design go back to Dutch craft, with emphasis on shallow draft, broad beam and a huge, gaff-rigged mainsail. Remarkable speed is a dividend. The ship's dimensions are: overall length 106 feet, beam 25 feet, draft 13 feet. The tonnage is 69 gross.

*Clearwater*'s hull is of wood and her single mast reaches up to 108 feet above the waterline. Poughkeepsie is the *Clearwater*'s home port. Her purpose has been to make known the importance of clean water and a clean environment. She is a resounding success and has done much for a cause that is now widely popular, although it was not so originally.

ABOVE: *The* Clearwater.

# Club Mediterranée

In recent years a number of ultramodern, highly computerized sailing vessels intended for the cruise trade have evolved. Extremely luxurious and quite successful, they are a special breed. One came over in 1976 and almost won the single-handed transatlantic race. She should get some mention here if for nothing more than her extraordinary look. The *Club Mediterranée* is probably the largest vessel ever designed for one person to sail. She is 236 feet long, has four masts, each with a jib and mainsail, and was built for Alain Colas, the winner of the 1972 single-handed transatlantic race sponsored by the London *Observer*.

BELOW: *The* Club Mediterranée.

# *Eendracht*

The *Eendracht,* a 118-foot-long topsail schooner, whose name means "union," was built in 1974 at the Cammenga Shipyard in Amsterdam. Her beam is 26 feet and she has a 12-foot draft. Her mainmast rises 112 feet above her waterline. She offers opportunities to young women as well as young men as trainees aboard her commodious decks. When it seemed that the ship would not be able to make her appearance at the 1976 OpSail, Levi Strauss &

Company, makers of the famous jeans known around the world, made a $50,000 contribution, asking only that the *Eendracht* have Levi-blue sails. To make sure that those who saw made the connection, the grateful Dutch sponsors of this fine vessel had a huge white pocket stitched on the blue mainsail.

ABOVE: *The* Eendracht.

# *Ernestina*

Built in Essex, Massachusetts, in 1894, the ship was well known as the exploration schooner *Effie M. Morrissey,* commanded by Captain Bob Bartlett, one of the last of a long line of Arctic explorers, from 1926 to 1945. When he died, his vessel was sold to some Grand Banks fishermen sailing out of the Cape Verde Islands off Africa. They renamed her *Ernestina.* After four decades of use, she was restored. She is 152 feet long, 25 feet wide and has a draft of 13 feet. Her mainmast rises 112 feet above the deck. She has 8000 square feet of sail and measures 120 gross tons. Her complement includes four officers and a crew of 11. The ship has a 210-horsepower diesel and can make eight knots.

BELOW: *The* Ernestina.

# *Freelance*

Built in 1907 at Clydebank, Scotland, the *Freelance* had a varied career, ending up in Antigua, West Indies, where, in 1976, a group of Antiguans were inspired to represent their fledgling nation at the American Bicentennial OpSail. The ship made a memorable appearance in the parade. The *Freelance* is a notable vessel in her own right, with a hull made of wrought iron. She measures 101 feet overall, has a beam of 19 feet and a draft of 13.6 feet. Her crew comes to 16, and she carries 25 trainees. With a sail area of 4000 square feet, this doughty old lady has a mainmast that rises 100 feet above the waterline.

ABOVE: *The* Freelance.

# *Harvey Gamage*

The *Harvey Gamage* is another of the truly beautiful replicas of American-style schooners. Like the *Bill of Rights,* she stands out among other craft wherever she sails, commanding attention as she heels in the wind and sweeps past. Both were built for the so-called "windjammer" cruise trade and both were built at the Harvey F. Gamage shipyard. New in 1973, the *Gamage* is named in appreciation of this master shipwright. She is 115 feet in length, 24 feet in beam, with a draft of ten feet. Her rig height is 91 feet for the mainmast and she has a sail area of 4200 square feet. Her wooden hull is white. A 120-horsepower diesel gives her a six-knot speed. She has recently been operated by the Dirigo Packet Co., of Clinton, Connecticut. Currently, she cruises in New England in the summer and in the Caribbean in the winter.

ABOVE: *The* Harvey Gamage.

# *Little Jennie*

Built in 1884, this Chesapeake Bay bugeye ketch is probably the second-oldest vessel in the American merchant marine. (The only one older is the schooner *Stephen Taber* of 1871, built at Glenwood, New York.) The *Little Jennie* was originally a commercial oyster boat. Designed and built by James T. Marsh, of Solomon's Island, Maryland, she has had a number of different careers, including rum runner during Prohibition and private yacht. She is currently a sail-training ship at Centerport, New York, having been saved from certain scrapping early in 1980 by Captain William Perks, who established Operation *Little Jennie*. Under his direction she was rebuilt so she could participate in the 1986 Operation Sail in New York. Since 1988 she has been under the aegis of The

Maritime Center on Long Island. Help is needed to continue the restoration of this example of a distinctive American ship type. In 1990, the *Little Jennie* was certified by the Coast Guard to carry 30 passengers. Her dimensions are: length 86 feet, beam 15.6 feet, draft three feet, five inches. She measures 28 tons gross and has a rig height of 60 feet. As a ketch, her foremast is taller than her mainmast, the opposite of the schooner rig. Her new diesel engine of 100 horsepower was acquired through the help of Peter Stanford, president of the National Maritime Historical Society.

---

ABOVE: *The* Little Jennie.

# *Petrel*

This lovely yawl has earned a place in maritime history by being the first commercially operated sailing ship to offer sails for a fee in New York waters, having begun the program in 1971. Built in 1938 to plans of Sparkman & Stephens, the *Petrel* was for a period a training ship for the Coast Guard Academy, New London, Connecticut. She participated in several of the famous Bermuda races from Newport. President John F. Kennedy sailed aboard her during this period. Then for a time she was run as a charter boat in the Caribbean. Captain Nick Van Nes took her over, brought her to New York, and began his pioneering work in New York harbor, sailing the 70-foot-long craft out of Lower Manhattan piers with 35 passengers on short afternoon and evening outings. She has a ten-foot beam, weighs 44 tons and boasts a 93-foot-tall mainmast with a small mizzen.

BELOW: *The* Petrel, *1979.*

# *Pioneer*

For thousands of fortunate people, this 105-year-old vessel, along with the *Petrel,* has given new meaning to the waters of New York harbor. For centuries the harbor was crowded with boats of all kinds loaded with people, many enjoying the sense of exhilaration that being on the water can give. Then most of this activity vanished, only the famed Circle Line and the marvelous Staten Island ferry remaining to carry on the traditions of Robert Fulton, John Stevens and Commodore Cornelius Vanderbilt. Acquired by the South Street Seaport Museum, the *Pioneer* runs afternoon and evening sails, reintroducing delighted New Yorkers to the splendors of the city's waters.

She can be said to be the last surviving iron-hulled vessel on the Atlantic coast (although, in the 1960s, she was replated with steel). Built at the Pioneer Iron Works, Marcus Hook, Pennsylvania, a product of the famous innovator John Roach, the *Pioneer* helped introduce iron to American shipbuilding. Her dimensions: overall length 102 feet, beam 22.6 feet, draft 4.6 feet. She has a tonnage of 43 gross and a sail area of 2707 feet. Her rig height is 76 feet. For many years she was operated as a cargo barge. Peter Stanford acquired her as a gift for South Street after she had been extensively restored as a private yacht. He first used her to take drug addicts out on two-week cruises, offering them what amounted to therapy. Many responded well to this daring campaign. In recent years the Seaport Museum's survival has required her use on a largely commercial basis. She was in both the 1976 and the 1986 tall-ship parades and remains the pride of South Street.

ABOVE: *The* Pioneer *in the 1978 Mayor's Cup Schooner Race, New York.*

# *Pride of Baltimore* and *Pride of Baltimore II*

In 1986, just days before she was to have led the parade into New York harbor, the *Pride of Baltimore* sank off Bermuda with considerable loss of life. She had been built in 1977 as a replica of the earliest Baltimore clippers, introduced well before the main clipper-ship era began. Before her tragic loss, she carried the fame of Baltimore overseas and was one of the best-used and best-known medium-sized private tall ships in the world. Of wooden construction, she had three officers and nine in the crew. As first built, the *Pride of Baltimore* was fitted with a topmast on the mainmast only.

This was altered when a taller topmast was fitted on the mainmast and the foremast was fitted with a topmast and a square yard, increasing the sail area to 9523 square feet. She was 136 feet long, had a 23-foot beam and a draft of ten feet. An 85-horsepower diesel was aboard. Her black hull was painted with a row of imitation gun ports. The *Pride of Baltimore II* was completed in 1988 and, by early 1990, had sailed 17,000 miles.

ABOVE: *The* Pride of Baltimore.

# *Providence*

Built in 1976, this is a replica of the 1760 American coastal cargo ship that is said to have fired the first naval cannon shots of the American Revolution. She was the first command of Captain John Paul Jones. The replica was built at Melville, Rhode Island, at the yard of John Brown (no connection with the famous shipbuilder in Scotland who built the *Queen Mary*). Some think she may be the only square-topsail sloop afloat at the moment. With a black and ivory fiberglass hull and real gun ports, she has a highly steeved bowsprit and a raised poop deck aft of the mast. This unusual-looking vessel is bigger than she looks, with an overall length of 110 feet. She is 22 feet wide and has a draft of ten feet. Her mast rises 97 feet above the deck and she offers 5000 square feet of sail area. The ship measures 59 gross tons. She requires three officers and a crew of two with five cadets.

ABOVE: *The* Providence.

# *Regina Maris*

The *Regina Maris* was built in 1908 for the Baltic cargo trade at the yard of J. Ring Anderson, Svendborg, Denmark. The rig height on the tallest of her seven masts is just over 100 feet. She has five square sails on her foremast and fore-and-aft sails on the other two. With an overall length of 150 feet, a beam of 26 feet and a draft of 11 feet, she measures 188 gross tons. Her oak hull is painted the traditional black. Her complement includes four officers, 30 crew and six cadets. At present the ship is laid up, seeking a new owner.

BELOW: *The* Regina Maris.

# Romance

The *Romance* was built in 1936 as the *Grethe,* and is another product of J. Ring Anderson. Originally she had no engine and sailed between Denmark, Greenland and Iceland. Surviving the war, she was used in the 1965 film *Hawaii,* for which she was renamed the *Thetis* and was sailed by Alan Villiers. For many years the *Romance* has been owned by Captain Arthur M. Kimberly. He has written that, since acquiring the brigantine in 1966, he has sailed her "more miles deepsea than any other privately-owned and operated square rigger in service today—125,000 miles of blue water voyaging, including two circumnavigations." All these miles were made with amateur crews of young people. The *Romance* has an overall length of 110 feet, a beam of 22 and a gross tonnage of 82 tons. Her sail area is 4500 square feet.

BELOW: *The* Romance.

# *Rose*

Built in 1970, this ship was designed as a replica of the British warship *Rose,* which blockaded the ports of Newport and Savannah during the American Revolution. Eventually scuttled off Savannah, she was one of the main reasons that the colonies decided to build an American navy. The State Assembly of Rhode Island took the lead in petitioning the new Congress to create a navy to "rid us of the *Rose.*" John Millar, who was responsible for the construction of the replica, went to the Smith-Rhuland yard at Lunenburg, Nova Scotia, to have his dream ship built, employing Philip Bolger as the designer. The *Rose* is 170 feet in length, 31 feet beam, 13 feet draft and has a sail area of 15,000 square feet. Originally, the replica had no auxiliary power. Later, when the ship became the responsibility of the H.M.S. *Rose* Foundation of Bridgeport, Connecticut, a 450-horsepower diesel engine was installed. In the 1976 and 1986 OpSails she carried 60 crew and trainees. The *Rose* later came under the supervision of Captain William F. Young, a retired Coast Guard officer who had been long active in the American Sail Training Association. His enthusiasm for Native American youth in New Mexico led to a new program. For 1991 it was planned that *Rose* take 12 to 14 Jémez Pueblo boys of 17 years of age on a working cruise through the Great Lakes, having included two in 1990. The Youngs have organized an outreach program for the Jémez, New Mexico, Community Presbyterian Church.

ABOVE: *The* Rose.

# *Santa María*

Countless replicas of the famous *Santa María* have been built. This one was begun in 1975 in St. Petersburg, Florida. She was built by John Budden, who planned to call her something like the *Young America*. But everyone else called her *Santa María* and eventually he yielded to popular opinion. Although no paintings or plans of the real *Santa María* have ever been found, the ship's overall dimensions are pretty well known. This replica has a length of 92 feet, including the short bowsprit. The beam is 19 feet and the draft only 7.6 feet. Her mainmast rises 60 feet above the waterline. The ship is built of wood stained brown. A very high poop and raised forecastle made the ship what has been called a "round ship." The great square sails had the Maltese cross as a decorative feature. A basketlike crow's nest on the main gives a sense of perspective to the whole ship, showing how small she really is.

ABOVE: *The* Santa María.

# Sea Cloud

This is one of the most palatial and largest square-rigged yachts ever built. In his *International Register of Historic Ships,* Norman Brouwer writes: "She was the only one built as a four-masted bark, and is today the only ship or bark-rigged yacht, built as such, in existence." Her original owners were E. F. Hutton, banker and playboy, and his wife, the former Marjorie Merriwether Post, heiress to the great Post Toasties family fortune. Hutton's two previous large yachts were both named *Hussar.* In 1930, Hutton went to Germany to have a third and still larger one built, choosing Germaniawerft in Kiel to do the job. His new giantess was completed in 1931.

Even in a day of big yachts, the *Sea Cloud*'s statistics were breathtaking. She was larger than J. P. Morgan's last steam yacht, *Corsair,* built at about the same time. The new *Hussar*'s length was 360 feet, with a beam of 50 feet and a draft of 17 feet. Her masts rose 188 feet above the waterline. With 29 sails she had a sail area of 32,000 square feet. Today she is the largest privately owned sailing ship in the world. Awarded to Mrs. Hutton in a divorce arrange-

ment, the vessel was renamed *Sea Cloud,* although a number of other names have been on her bows during her colorful career. Mrs. Hutton wed Joseph Davies, later Franklin D. Roosevelt's ambassador to the Soviet Union. The *Sea Cloud* became the "diplomatic palace" of the United States in Leningrad. After wartime service she fell into the hands of dictator Rafael Trujillo of the Dominican Republic and his son. Fortunately the ship and her exquisite interior work survived through years of misuse and a long period of idleness at Panama. In 1974 a group of Hamburg shipowners came to her rescue; her career has been "golden" ever since. Again the *Sea Cloud,* restored and brought back to a brilliant state of posh and polish, is run by Windjammer Segeltouristik. Thirty-seven cabins offer space for only 67 passengers. A job in the crew of 60 is considered among the most desirable jobs aboard any ship today.

BELOW: *The bedroom of the* Sea Cloud*'s owner's suite no. 2.* OPPOSITE: *The* Sea Cloud.

# *Shenandoah*

The *Shenandoah* was launched in 1964, having been built after the design of the 1849 U.S. Revenue cutter *Joseph Lane.* Possibly the climax of the career of builder Harvey F. Gamage, this magnificent ship was built for passenger charter service, in which she has had great success. She makes Vineyard Haven, Massachusetts her home port. From the beginning, Captain Robert S. Douglas has been her captain and is the guiding force of the Coastwise Packet Co., her owners. She is a two-masted topsail schooner with a length of 152 feet, a beam of 23 feet and a draft of 11 feet. Her sail area comes to 6788 square feet and her mainmast rises 94 feet above the waterline. In printed materials, Captain Douglas notes that the ship is "the only non auxiliary, square rigged vessel operating under the American flag." She was built for a crew of eight and 37 passengers, since cut to 29. There are two four-berth cabins, four three-berth cabins, four two-berth cabins and one single. Every cabin has a porthole or skylight. All are "small, but snug." None has running water, but all have atmosphere. The main saloon is decorated with "a brass ship's clock, two long gimbaled mahogany tables, hanging kerosene lamps, two racks of brass hilted Union naval cutlasses, ship portraits, a stove and pump organ."

ABOVE: *The* Shenandoah.

# *Sherman Zwicker*

When launched in 1942, this vessel was the largest of the Nova Scotian fishing vessels. Known as the "leviathan of the fleet," she had been built by the Smith and Rhuland yard in Lunenburg, a firm founded in 1789. Sherman Zwicker was the head of the fishing company that built her. Each year she would make three trips to the Grand Banks. The ship has an overall length of 142 feet, a beam of 26 feet and a draft of 13 feet. Her mainmast rises 95 feet above the deck. Her wooden hull is painted black. An auxiliary diesel of 320 horsepower gives her a ten-knot speed. She requires six officers and a crew of 20 and can carry six cadets. Her last fishing trip was in 1968, when she went to Labrador. Retired, she has become the chief exhibit at the Grank Banks Schooner Museum, Boothbay, Maine.

ABOVE: *The* Sherman Zwicker.

# St. Lawrence II

This large brigantine was built by the Kingston Shipyards, Ltd., in Kingston, Ontario. Although she was launched in December 1953, she was not commissioned until July 1957. Her owners are the Royal Canadian Sea Cadet Corps, operating under the name of Brigantine Incorporated. The Sea Cadet Corps were organized in Ontario to train boys between the ages of 13 and 18 "to live in a restricted space as a community in which one member is dependent on the other." The training period is only 15 days, and those who do well are given a second and even a third training assignment. Eventually, if they show real aptitude, they become members of the ship's permanent crew. The 34-gross-ton vessel was named after the original *St. Lawrence,* a 112-cannon three-decker built in 1814 by the Navy Shipyard at Point Frederick, Kingston, Canada. The present craft has an overall length, including bowsprit, of 73 feet, a beam of 15 feet and a draft of eight feet. Her mainmast rises 53 feet above the waterline. She has a complement of eight officers and can carry 18 cadets. The vessel has a sail area of 2490 square feet and is equipped with a 72-horsepower diesel.

BELOW: *The* St. Lawrence.

# Stephen Taber

The *Stephen Taber* was christened and slipped into the waters of Hempstead Harbor in October 1871. She is the oldest ship documented in continuous service in the American merchant marine. A local reporter of the day noted, "the schooner *Stephen Taber* was launched from the yard of Mr. Bedel, Glenwood, on Thurs. of last week. She is a well built, natty schooner—she bears a good name and no doubt will prove a profitable investment for all concerned." She has certainly done all that, maintaining her full-sail status in the process, and is still in profitable service. Named after a member of one of Long Island's famous Taber family, she has her home port in Camden, Maine, and is regularly advertised with a number of other so-called "windjammers" in the travel section of the *New York Times*. Each Monday from June to September she sails on week-long cruises out of Camden with a crew of six and up to 23 passengers. When he rebuilt her in 1981, her owner, Captain Kenneth ("O.K.") Barnes, and his wife Ellen anticipated at least another century of service for the sturdy wooden-hulled vessel. The schooner's dimensions: length, 68 feet; beam, 22 feet; tonnage 47, gross.

ABOVE: *The* Stephen Taber.

# *Tiki*

Serving out of Boothbay, Maine, this lovely white schooner was built in 1932. The 78-gross-ton craft is 105 feet in overall length, has a beam of 20 feet and a draft of ten feet. A 1200-horsepower diesel engine gives her a speed of nine knots. She has a mast height of 110 feet and sail area of 3500 square feet. She usually operates with four officers and four crew members, and can accommodate 20 cadets. Built from a design by John Alden, this handsome craft has had a distinguished career. She once featured in a television series. The upper part of her white hull is usually decorated with a light blue line. She has traditional anchors with old-style stocks, marking her as designed for sail training. Following the traditional design of the late-nineteenth-century American schooner, the *Tiki*'s bowsprit continues the same lines of the hull proper, rising only slightly. Her sheer is moderate and her sails are attached to the masts with old-style wooden hoops. Her wheel is out in the open, far aft, just abaft a low charthouse, the only superstructure the ship has.

Above: *The* Tiki.

# *Unicorn*

The *Unicorn* was built in Finland in 1948. She has a length of 140 feet overall, a beam of 243 feet and a draft of only nine feet. Her tonnage is 190 gross. She looks much larger from bow on than she really is because of the panoply of square sails on her foremast. Captain Jacques R. Thiry bought her in 1970 and restored her almost single-handedly. He brought her to New York in the fall of 1973, and she stayed at the South Street Seaport Museum through the 1976 festivities. After 1976 she was used on Long Island Sound for a season by Captain Louis Bejarano, attracting large crowds. She is perhaps the finest of the group of medium-sized square-rigged ships that came to America for the Bicentennial and have remained.

ABOVE: *The* Unicorn.

# *Westward* and *Corwith Cramer*

The *Westward,* run by the Sea Educational Association (SEA), is a staysail schooner built in 1960 in Germany. With headquarters at Woods Hole, Massachusetts, SEA is a nonprofit group that has had students from over 220 colleges attend its sea-semester program. Designed by Eldredge and McInnis, the *Westward* was constructed in Germany by Aberking & Rasmussen as a North Sea pilot schooner. Her dimensions are: overall length 125 feet; beam 22 feet; and draft 12 feet. Her sail area totals 7000 square feet. Not only does she teach 125 sea-semester students a year, but she collects oceanographic information for some 20 different scientists and research institutions. Her complement includes seven officers, 21 students and an assortment of research people for e[...] cruise. In 1988, she was completely rebuilt. A compan[...] the *Westward,* the *Corwith Cramer,* was completed in [...] ship is named after the founder, long the guiding spi[...] organization. She is 135 feet long and has a sail area of 780[...] feet. A brigantine, she was built in Bilbao, Spain. A typical y[...] see each of these beautiful schooners make six cruises of abo[...] nautical miles.

BELOW, LEFT AND RIGHT: *The* Westward.

# Young America

This 100-ton brigantine, having started life with much fanfare, may have come to a premature end. She was built by Captain David N. Kent, of Port Jefferson, New York, in 1975 to be a part of the 1976 Operation Sail. An innovative designer and builder, Captain Kent made her of ferrocement. She attracted attention from her keel laying to her gala first appearance on Long Island Sound. Captain Kent created the Port Jefferson Packet Co., Inc., to operate her, and was her master in the Bicentennial parade. The vessel, with an overall length of 130 feet, a 26-foot beam and a draft of nine feet, was christened *Enchantress*. She was distinguished by a dark green hull and 5660 square feet of sail. Her full complement numbered 76, including cadets. The vessel had a mast height of 118 feet above the waterline. In 1980 she was operated by the Long Island Nautical Festival under the name of *Young America*. Then she was taken over by two nonprofit groups, one of which ran her on short cruises out of Miami. The other group, which planned to use her at Atlantic City, was poorly financed; the lovely vessel has been allowed to deteriorate. When she was last spotted, at Gardiner's Basin, Atlantic City, her status was described by someone in authority as "out of commission."

ABOVE: *The* Young America.